THE BLUE CLOWN

THE BLUE CLOWN
Dialogues

By
Augusto Centeno y Rilova
and
Donald Sutherland

University of Nebraska Press · Lincoln

Publishers on the Plains

UNP

Copyright © 1971 by the University of Nebraska Press

International Standard Book Number 0–8032–0791–3

Library of Congress Catalog Card Number 76–132835

Manufactured in the United States of America

To E.D.C.

Contents

Prologue

A. C. R.

. . . .

D. S.

You make conversation between us more difficult than ever, Augusto, having died on Christmas morning of 1965. That is more implacable a silence than your refusal to speak to me at any time since our last quarrel, in 1958.

A. C. R.

. . . . .

D. S.

But you still do speak, and volubly, in the memories of your thousands of students. And among the few papers you left I find a plan, full of your manner, for a collection of dialogues you never wrote, on Being, on Solitudes, on the Theatre, on Cultures, and so on; I can imagine what they would have sounded like, their pitch and phrasing. How I wish you had written them! How I want those potential dialogues to exist!

A. C. R.

. . . .

D. S.

Some were to be dialogues between a master and his disciple, between a Don Rafael, a retired professor, as you lately were, and a Marcelino, a former student of his. For many years we were master and disciple, though we could quarrel and not speak for ten years on end. So perhaps I could write at least the part of Marcelino, though I am not a Spaniard and was not a good disciple.

A. C. R.

. . . . .

D. S.

How can I help writing those dialogues, even your part as Don Rafael, remembering your hoarse voice and much of how you thought, in sharp clear tones?

A. C. R.

. . . . .

D. S.

You did say once that, in the composition of ideas, you were an architect and I only a bricklayer. The plans I have of yours are terrifyingly slight for a mere bricklayer to follow, so the structure may well collapse. Dare I still try?

A. C. R.

. . . . .

D. S.

You are not much help—and knowing as you do my way of indecision—Enough! I shall have to make up my own mind, and even yours.

A. C. R.

. . . . !

D. S.

No, but you do help. I find in your notes a quotation from Giordano Bruno, carefully copied out word by word and even letter by letter, like a sacred text:

"It is better to be than not to be; it is more worthy to create what is good than not to create it. To posit [create] being and truth is incomparably better than to allow not-being or nothing."

They cannot have burned him for that. And at least I shall not, in this case of your dialogues, allow not-being.

A. C. R.

. . . . .

D. S.
Hasta la vista.

A. C. R.

. . . . .

FOUR DIALOGUES ON TO BE

TIME: 196–

PLACE: *An open patio in Colorado. A view of the Rockies looking reasonably like the Guadarrama or the Sierra Nevada.*

PERSONS: *DON RAFAEL. An Andalusian, part Castilian, who has remained Spanish but, because of the régime, returns to Spain only in memory. A retired professor of Spanish and Esthetics. As old as the century. Blind. A Greco face.*

MARCELINO. A cross-bred American with Spanish prejudices and training. Once a student of Don Rafael, now a retired professor, but of Greek and Latin. Good eyes. Bad memory. A broader face.

They sit in garden chairs by a table on which there are a few books, a notebook, drinks, olives, and peanuts.

Dialogue One

DON RAFAEL

Son, I have made up my mind. Being is one.

MARCELINO

Sir, perhaps it is.

DON RAFAEL

No perhaps. Being is one. I have made up my mind.

MARCELINO

And changed it, Don Rafael. You may change it again.

DON RAFAEL

Which would only be my duty as an intellectual, to change when the truth changes. But this one does not change. When did I ever not think Being is one? I have always thought so, and now I am more entirely certain. That is all. More intensely certain.

MARCELINO

Thirty years ago you would have said perhaps Being is one; or that it is many; or heterogeneous; or indefinite; perhaps.

DON RAFAEL

Never.

MARCELINO

Once at least. Thirty years ago, when you

were a young teacher and I was your student, we went together to a lecture by Professor Lovejoy. Do you remember him?

DON RAFAEL

I can see him now. He looks like a stunted eagle.

MARCELINO

So he did. Do you remember his lecture?

DON RAFAEL

Not a syllable. But yes—it must have been about his specialty, *The Great Chain of Being*.

MARCELINO

It was. It began with Parmenides, and after an hour we were not much past Parmenides, and Being was still one. It made us both very restless. We felt the Great Chain acutely, if not the Being.

DON RAFAEL

You were in Greek. If Parmenides made you restless it must have been because I was restless.

MARCELINO

Very likely. In those days I had not much mind of my own.

DON RAFAEL

More than what you have now, my poor Marcelino, after decades of Positivism and studying other minds in books.

MARCELINO

Well, Don Rafael, perhaps I was less academic then. At least I was more ignorant. But, in fact, what was it that made us so restless?

4

DON RAFAEL

Certainly not, as you seem to think now, the idea that Being is one. It must have been that Lovejoy, a great historian of ideas, treated the idea as an historical fact, a safe object for scholarship. It is more, it is presently and urgently true or not true, to be dealt with personally. It is not an exhibit in a museum but a bull in a ring. Just as religion, for better or worse, cannot be contained in the history of theology. Removing the unity of Being to the fifth century B.C.—with all due respect for that very good century of yours—would have made me restless in my youth.

MARCELINO

It would make you even more restless now, and me too, now that I have retired from the fifth century.

DON RAFAEL

High time.

MARCELINO

Perhaps too late.

DON RAFAEL

"Not dead, enough said."

MARCELINO

That is Gertrude Stein, being as simply complete and pointed as Seneca.

DON RAFAEL

Great Spanish writers, both of them. But we have also a more bodily and harsher manner. On the table you will find a notebook with a leather cover.

MARCELINO

Yes.

5

DON RAFAEL

On the third page I scribbled something yesterday. Perhaps you can read it.

MARCELINO

It looks like part of a dialogue.

DON RAFAEL

Well?

MARCELINO

"Either you think of culture as capital producing dividends, or else as wages to be earned every day, and spent."

"Meaning what?"

"You can store tons of wheat in silos, but you cannot store the loaves of bread. We ask to be given our *daily* bread."

"How does scholarship come into this?"

"Scholarship busies itself with counting, measuring, comparing the loaves of bread kept in its silos. Of course the bread is very hard, but it doesn't matter. It is not expected to be eaten."

DON RAFAEL

How do you like the interlocutor?

MARCELINO

Not at all. He is impertinent.

DON RAFAEL

Exactly. Plato would have done better to use him.

MARCELINO

Well, so much for scholarship, if not for Plato. But thirty years ago you had other objections to Lovejoy than his scholarship and you told him so after the lecture. He was venerable; you were young; as an inter-

6

locutor you wound up deferentially, saying that perhaps your objections were a little Romantic.

DON RAFAEL
And what did he say?

MARCELINO
He said yes, they were very Romantic.

DON RAFAEL
Did he smile, do you remember?

MARCELINO
I remember he did not. He did not live up to the name Lovejoy. Nor up to Parmenides, who could be playful, and snow even Socrates. In spite of the odd sportiveness of its originator, I have always thought Being a serious matter, whether one, many, or imaginary, and yet the solemnity of Lovejoy made me restless.

DON RAFAEL
You forget how serious you were at the time, and how genuinely solemn. The wars were coming. No, it was Lovejoy who was not serious. Reducing such an idea to history!

MARCELINO
Well, the history of ideas was in fashion in those days. And quite lively. It certainly kept everybody busy. There was even a journal about it.

DON RAFAEL
Which is why we lost Spain and almost the whole war. Only the very worst ideas, the worst of German ideas, were on the loose and had their mobility; the best were being busily stored away in history, a kind of Maginot Line.

MARCELINO

We did not know that then, either of us. It seemed a harmless and very pleasant fashion. Intellectual fashions are a kind of daily bread, say what you will. Your technical objection to Lovejoy was fashionable too: he made little of Indefinite Becoming and far too much of Concluded Being.

DON RAFAEL

Not in those terms. They would have been German.

MARCELINO

Werden and *Sein?* No, you would not have used them even in translation. But you made some such opposition of terms.

DON RAFAEL

You see what a memory you have! It is bad enough to be blind, but to have a disciple with amnesia! What if the Evangelists had been like you?

MARCELINO

Perhaps you set Existence against Being?

DON RAFAEL

It would have been a mistake and I would not have made it, even if I had heard of Sartre. That Alsatian pedant!

MARCELINO

You had heard of Heidegger, a worse pedant and a German.

DON RAFAEL

I had even read him. But how could I have used his ideas? *Sein und Zeit!* What an underestimation of Time! What abject passivity!

8

MARCELINO

Still, I don't think your opposing terms would have come from your teacher, Unamuno, that basic and predatory Basque. He just pirated Being, seized it for his own Existence: "I exist; therefore I am." I like the gesture, but that is not the kind of Being that Lovejoy was ever so objectively and deferentially talking about.

DON RAFAEL

No. Don Miguel was thinking perhaps too informally, with his tragic sense, making everything a matter of Life and Death. But just for that reason, he was taking Being more seriously than Lovejoy did.

MARCELINO

Perhaps you objected in terms of Life, then, or, as you liked to say at the time, "Livingness."

DON RAFAEL

Vivencia. Yes, that was probably what I had in mind, whatever the word was I may have used in English. Not "Livingness." It did not yet exist in philosophical jargon. Lovejoy would have thought it Romantic, or the kind of word an artistic lady might use.

MARCELINO

It still conveys more sentiment than sense. Could you find no ordinary or dry English word for *vivencia?*

DON RAFAEL

Since it is your language, you must know a great beauty of English is in how everybody has been able to do what he likes with it, at least from Chaucer on, and invent words when the regular language fails. Spanish is not so tractable. If "livingness" is bad, *vivencia* is worse. Ortega y Gasset had to invent it because there was no word in Spanish for *Erlebnis*. Antonio Machado, a regular mossback when it came to language, made fun of it at the time and even parodied it in his own word, *videncia*.

MARCELINO
Well, *vivencia* is no longer a neologism. I have heard it used quite casually.

DON RAFAEL
In academic circles, and after half a century! Between ourselves, let us forget philology.

MARCELINO
How can we? These days it has devoured philosophy. I do not mean exactly what you do by "livingness," which does not mean exactly *vivencia*, or what Ortega meant by it when you got it from him in Madrid. And *vivencia* does not exactly translate *Erlebnis* or *Lebendigkeit*, or whatever Dilthey meant by either word when Ortega got it from him by way of Berlin or Marburg. I suppose Dilthey isolated the notion of *Erlebnis* or *Lebendigkeit* from what was implicit in Nietzsche's disjunction of History from Life, but would it have been one of Nietzsche's ideas exactly? Probably not, because for Dilthey Life is still no more than the substance of History, or the processive as against the finished aspect of fact. Or did he get *Erlebnis* out of Schleiermacher and theological enthusiasm? That would get us into German Romanticism at its deepest.

DON RAFAEL
Enough! More than enough! Let us stop short at Nietzsche! You are not going to tell me you have read Schleiermacher!

MARCELINO
Only a little.

10

DON RAFAEL

You see what scholarship has brought you to. But are you suggesting that our idea, our ideas, of "livingness" are German after all? Are you, after what we have just been saying, trying to reduce the idea to its history?

MARCELINO

I must have been, out of habit. I was brought up on "influences." My apologies.

DON RAFAEL

Never mind. What you traced was not history so much as genealogy. Nietzsche is perhaps the great-grandfather of my idea, but it is not his idea. The idea, even as you describe its vicissitudes, is a distinctly different idea in each generation, leading a life of its own, though a family resemblance may persist throughout. Even if it did not emigrate and change its name, as in this case it has done, it would still change in each generation, and in each mind of the same generation. By this time there is no word in German, that I know of, for "livingness." *Erlebnis* has too much the meaning of "experience" and *Lebendigkeit* too much that of "liveliness." We can afford a German side to our ancestry, especially as that side is a nobility, and so long as we are not on speaking terms with it, and so long as we have other grandfathers and great-grandfathers from loftier nobilities and to spare.

MARCELINO

There must be a good many Greeks in our tree, and Romans. And they had the same trouble over words. *To on* or *to eon* and *ousia* were neologisms and very wretched Greek, not to mention the variabilities of meaning; *ens, essentia, entitas,* are insufferable Latin.

DON RAFAEL

Young man, are you ever going to remember what I said to Lovejoy?

MARCELINO

Compadre, it doesn't look much like it. But certainly you said something vitalistic.

DON RAFAEL

Vitalistic! I? Did I?

MARCELINO

I don't mean that you spoke from a school or a tradition of nineteenth-century Vitalism or the dead end of it in Bergson—I mean you spoke personally from some acute sense of life, and I felt much the same way. We were young, with our lives around us and ahead of us, and we probably felt that Being—at least as Lovejoy described it— was a restraint or an obstruction.

DON RAFAEL

There you have it!

MARCELINO

Have what?

DON RAFAEL

That Being remains what it is, but we change, so its relations change and its value changes. That is why I have had to make up my mind about what I already knew.

MARCELINO

Excuse me, Don Rafael. I don't see exactly what has changed.

DON RAFAEL

Our livingness has. You just finished saying we were young, with our lives ahead of us, and Being seemed an obstruction. Now, obviously, we are old, most of our lives are behind us, and Being is not an obstruction, not to our present livingness.

MARCELINO
Then what is it?

DON RAFAEL
Let me think. Fix my drink, will you? And how is yours?

MARCELINO
About gone.

DON RAFAEL
Shall we say Being is terminal?

MARCELINO
Why not? We ourselves are getting to be that.

DON RAFAEL
Young man, behave yourself. Be a good pedant and give me a serious answer. *Salud!* But an answer, not a bibliography.

MARCELINO
Salud! As a good pedant I could only tell you what Aristotle would say to such a question, which is roughly yes, or what Plato would say, which is roughly no. About the question itself a pedant would be indifferent, or at best light-minded. At worst, authoritarian.

DON RAFAEL
Then can you, personally and not pedantically, be serious about Being?

MARCELINO
I am afraid not, or not very, though I still think Being is very serious and I can be seriously interested in questions about it.

DON RAFAEL
I don't know what you mean by that. Do you?

MARCELINO
Nearly. Like many late classical people, like the Skeptics, like Diderot, I prefer the activity of speculation to anything I might decide is truth. If Being turned out to be a truth and a good thing, as an American I might want to acquire it, but even more I might want to do something with it. With proper conversion and promotion it might be nearly as marketable in this country as God. But if it is terminal and final I suppose there is nothing profitable to be done with it except contemplate it, and that does not interest me much. As a Spaniard, now, with a whole collection of major saints and mystics in your ancestry, you would find the mere contemplation of Being completely interesting. And that does interest me very much.

DON RAFAEL
As a student of Spain?

MARCELINO
No.

DON RAFAEL
As a student of mine?

MARCELINO
That may have started it, but I am mainly interested as a student of what different people do with their lives, or do about Being, from one country to another. I have taken up a mild form of diplomacy or public relations—writing plays—so mine is a practical interest, perfectly American, and far from disinterested.

DON RAFAEL
What makes you think the Spanish are so

14

disinterestedly interested? Contemplation is never quite enough for us. It is true that we can go to sleep for a hundred years or so, as the country seems to be doing now, but even our dreams are active and violent. Ours is a sleep of conquerors, whether it be of Mexico or of the Kingdom of God. Contemplation was not enough for my great-aunt Teresa of Avila or for Uncle John of the Cross. Certainly not for Don Quijote, who might as well be an ancestor, and even the contemplations of Saint Ignatius are "exercises" for a military order of corpses. You can imagine, if you haven't read them, how stimulating they necessarily are. Not that we have anything at all to do with your undisciplined and aimless Pragmatism. Our actions, or rather our exploits, are always closely and severely related to an absolute, to Being.

MARCELINO
Or to a reverse absolute, Not-Being, or Death, or Nada. Good, but I do not feel that urgent or that polarized about anything.

DON RAFAEL
Then how in the world can you expect to write plays? And how, as a student of mine, can you not be vitally interested in Being?

MARCELINO
Because it is so final.

DON RAFAEL
Ah! So you do say it is?

MARCELINO
Well, I will say I say so, in spite of the many objections, theological and historical. It is at least the final abstraction one can make in logic, and its finality was certainly something we felt about it when listening to Professor Lovejoy.

15

DON RAFAEL

And still do. We agree on that one point, whether or not we like the finality, whether or not we are equal to it. We are not aspiring to know Being "in modeless mode" as some saints aspired to know God, but only to consider this one mode. We are not saying, as I suppose we might, that Being is finality, but that it is final and that finality is one of its modes. And that its finality manifests itself in many finalities of this world.

MARCELINO

Agreed. You sound like a bishop, Don Rafael, but pray go on.

DON RAFAEL

A cardinal, if you don't mind. A cardinal would say perfection instead of finality. But to oblige you I shall call Being not final or perfect, but concluded.

MARCELINO

I like the sound of it, as if it would stay put. Not put away, but just put.

DON RAFAEL

You are growing old, my son. Its concluded-ness was the trouble with it when we were young, more trouble than finality, since many more things are concluded than are at all final. When life is ahead of us we do not care to think that everything we do or leave unfinished or undone is a foregone conclusion, that our freedom, our adventures, our creation of novelties, will all disappear into their results, or their lack of results, into conclusions, in short, into Being. Even if we naively imagine we are in time going to be something or do something perfect, we do not consider that that something, as perfect, would by definition be also finished. But when most of our life is behind us, or finished, we then ask what has become of it or

16

where it is. We do not want to see it lost, or irreparably receding or vanished like the *neiges d'antan*. Finished should be complete and acquired, not lost. We want it to stay with us as much as possible, in souvenirs that are still present, in records, letters, monuments, memories, anything of it that still is and reassures us the past really was, really had being of some kind.

MARCELINO

Do you feel that way about it? I never do, not yet. I know it is inane for people to say as they do that you cannot live in the past. Of course you can, and for many people it is the only tense of time fit for human habitation. But I am not there yet.

DON RAFAEL

I often am. Look in my notebook again, will you? About the middle, under a heading "The Artist and Life."

MARCELINO

Yes. Here: "The past is beautiful because it is complete. No matter whether it is full to the brim with joy, sorrow, happiness, etc. Its completeness is its beauty. The present, let us say the last moment, whether positive or negative, of today having been something before quite turning into tomorrow, possesses the value of adding a little more enchantment to the past.

"The future is God's. We have nothing to do with it until it begins to approach on the horizon, turning into the present. Until that last moment, the future is unknowable, meaningless, uninteresting, inhuman. To live oriented toward the future instead of the past seems to me to live backwards.

"I don't know what this religious, aesthetic perspective can be called. Does it coincide with, approach, combat, any of the historical positions? Have no idea.

17

"*The Leopard* succeeded, I believe, in expressing this point of view. Of course the ending is sad. Why not? And it will be a long time before a new life can begin to produce its own complete past, to turn again into its own sadness."

DON RAFAEL
Well?

MARCELINO
Very beautiful, Sir. I respond to the feeling, irresistibly, but it is, as I said, not mine.

DON RAFAEL
And the ideas?

MARCELINO
Like almost all ideas, they articulate a particular intuition or feeling, and perhaps one should ask no more, but separated from the feeling, they will not stand up. Take Dante's "No greater grief than remembering the happy times when one is in misery." Francesca no doubt feels that way, and the remark is true to her feeling, but there are plenty of greater griefs. One is that of Helen of Troy in Homer, who is uncertain that the happy past really existed at all. You may say in the abstract that the past is complete, every bit of it was, even if the historians have not written it all up, but the real terror is that as a matter of feeling, of memory, it is not complete. One cannot remember all of it or even be sure one remembers a little of it as it really was.

DON RAFAEL
You are still very young, my son. You no doubt aspire to a complete and rounded future, to success, in a word, but soon you will do as I sometimes do, aspire to a complete and rounded past.

18

MARCELINO

How about a complete and rounded present?
Once I felt there was such a thing. Have you ever felt, as
someone has, that the past is only the excrement of actual
living?

DON RAFAEL

Perhaps, briefly, when I was about thirty.
But any of these tenses can be exaggerated, I admit. A
natural fondness for the past can become a mania. Even a
whole culture, like ours, so advanced it is senile, and with
the end at hand every day, can go into a perfect frenzy for
archaeology, even for the remotest prehistory, and millions
upon millions of your almighty dollars go into it. If the
world, by a technology oriented on the future, is going to
have a very short future and cease within our lifetime to
go on being, at least we can assure ourselves that it will
really have been, and in very large quantities and extents,
very nearly complete. So the past, as one mode of the
concludedness of Being, in its factual and museum manifestations at least, becomes for us a preservative and not
an obstruction, a reassurance and not a menace to our
livingness.

MARCELINO

I suppose it does. But are we, after all,
rehabilitating history?

DON RAFAEL

No. Or only insofar as it subserves our
livingness. When it impedes, we reject it.

MARCELINO

Well, in theory at least, Being is less a matter
of the past or the future than of the present—an eternal
present as they like to say when they are not saying

19

timeless. The present is constantly "in being," while the past no longer is and the future, permanently, is not yet. Memories and projects "are" only in the present. A philosopher might also say that the present is one, a single point or span or aspect of duration for everybody, while the past and future are, now, multiple, wildly variable, and even reversible in the imaginations of everybody. So if the present is pretty well one and Being has anything much to do with it, Being might be, as you say, one, and even better, unifying, since all things presently existing are unified by being present, as all beings may be logically unified by sharing in Being.

DON RAFAEL
Theoretically, schematically, by the clock, that may be so, but if the present . . .

MARCELINO
A cardinal would say actuality . . .

DON RAFAEL
. . . if the present is a primary mode of Being, one gets different values on that too, quite aside from the concrete situations of the present, which can be painful or delightful. In one's youth the present in general is constantly preliminary, either an encumbrance or a springboard for one's rush into the future. In age one instinctively does not rush into the future, where there is Death. One tries, besides preserving the past, to immobilize the present, to treasure it or at least to slow it down.

MARCELINO
That must be ordinarily if not universally true. I remember when I was young it seemed to me that everything around me was standing still and I was the only thing perceptibly in motion. Then suddenly when I was about thirty-five I noticed that younger people were

launching themselves at incredible rates of speed into careers and adventures and trajectories, while other people were more rapidly than usual growing old, and I had a feeling I was standing still. Naturally I was not, but that was the feeling, and I suppose that at that time, if I had thought of it, Being would have been neither an obstruction nor a preservative, but just a fact in itself or a location, as if I had reached my state of perfection in a world which was fundamentally complete. What nonsense!—but such is livingness, and it must presume or project many more aspects of Being in the course of a lifetime even than these. For Unamuno in his prime, Being was not something just given or occurring of itself, but something to be anticipated, dragged into the present by main force.

DON RAFAEL

If we take everybody and their lifetimes into account, the aspects become all but infinite. Many young people consume the present and neglect the future, for fear of being thirty, and many old people are astonishingly full of projects. And I suppose it is the future, not the past, that the dying think of, whatever they may imagine it contains.

MARCELINO

Cato started to learn Greek when he was eighty; Alice Toklas, when eighty-eight, finally gave up smoking because, she said, it wasn't getting her anywhere.

DON RAFAEL

Remind me of that. It is a perfect example of a difference between livingness and life. Life after all coheres with its conditions; livingness does not, or need not, having a willfulness, a grace, a gayety, a *traje de luces*.

MARCELINO

So livingness, not life, would be naturally opposed to Being?

DON RAFAEL

I don't think so. But that would depend on what we decide to mean by Being.

MARCELINO

For that, let me improve our drinks. What a decision! Laura Riding once frightened a young professor of English very badly by taking hold of his knee and asking him what he meant by Being. He probably meant nothing by it at all, but even if he had been a professor of philosophy he could have been as frightened, or more so, knowing how many versions of Being there are—from pure Motion to pure Stasis. And it can be made to include almost anything, or any aspect of anything, or everything, if you fiddle with it enough.

DON RAFAEL

Like God.

MARCELINO

Yes, as in Deism or Pantheism. But let us not entangle ourselves in heresies.

DON RAFAEL

No, nor in orthodoxies. Let us leave God out of it for a while, though He too is One.

MARCELINO

By courtesy. But the best reason for leaving Him out is that if we did get Him mixed up with Being, He would give an authority and absolute value to Being, certainly a fixed value to its modes, and we seem to have decided already that at least two of those modes, finality and actuality, have a highly variable value, from one person to another and from one age to another within the single lifetime.

DON RAFAEL

I think you like to dwell on complications, to

22

make sure of not having to make up your mind. But if we leave God out, so as not to prejudice Being toward absolute and imperative value, why not leave people out as well, so as not to prejudice it toward relative and optional value?

MARCELINO
Yes, why not? If we left God and people and value out we would be objective.

DON RAFAEL
We would even be logicians or scientists!

MARCELINO
Is there any harm in that, so long as we don't make it a habit?

DON RAFAEL
No. But we will only be amateurs.

MARCELINO
Good. And we will ask only the most rudimentary questions.

DON RAFAEL
Good. Here is one for you, the most rudimentary I can think of: is there any such thing as Being?

MARCELINO
Well, Don Rafael, there has been. For the Greeks there was such a thing, and their questions were rather about where Being is, outside the physical universe or inside it or somehow radiating into it from outside. Those questions kept everybody nicely occupied for a few thousand years, and then we had Kant, and the questions became, not for the first time but very decisively, whether Being was inside the *mind* or outside. On the whole it was a projection from inside the mind toward a dubious out-

23

side, but inside or out Kant called it an empty concept, or the emptiest. Well, if it had no interest or reality outside the human mind it still had a great deal of interest and reality in the human mind, since much human action was about it; if there was no absolute in the universe there certainly was in human history, so everybody got interested in history, past, present, or yet to come. History itself became an absolute, final and as actual as anybody could make it.

DON RAFAEL
Does that bring us up to date?

MARCELINO
Just about. The Existentialists are usually not interested in history, and live in a religious perspective, whether God is present or absent. But they do make much of Being, interpreted as almost anything external to the mind, which tends in turn to be a negativity or Nothingness. And there we are.

DON RAFAEL
Very clever. You have managed to resume the history of the idea of Being without a trace of the intelligence, the passion, the sheer work that have gone into it for thousands of years. I don't believe in being docile toward history, but one should at least have some human piety toward what was once its livingness.

MARCELINO
I was not being clever. I was just trying to be objective.

DON RAFAEL
And you see where that gets us. To a choice between triviality and subjectivity. Subjectively, then, I

am. Within this very moment I am final. I am actual. I am one.

MARCELINO

So you appear to be to me, Don Rafael, all but objectively. You have, as they say, *mucho ser*. And intensity of presence, and integrity and, for me, authority. But all that is seen from the outside, by me. Subjectively, from inside you, all you say must be doubtful.

DON RAFAEL

No. Not unless I go about cultivating doubts for the sheer philosophy of it. I do not say my being is a given thing, though I might say my bare existence is. My being is an act of Will or, as they say in law, an act of presence. It is my creation, my assertion if you like, an assumption for all my further acts of living, and as arbitrary as you please, but there is no doubt about it. It is. For better or for worse, it is.

MARCELINO

In my case it is not quite so. I don't think I am pure negativity or Not-Being, or pure anything for that matter, but it is only outside me that I find Being at all clear or convincing.

DON RAFAEL

You have already said as much. If you are not directly interested in Being, your Will to Be is necessarily slack. You are uncinctured to the point of unsightliness. At least you will admit you exist?

MARCELINO

Gladly. And so do you. As men of flesh and bone, we should have some cheese and crackers. And I see our wives coming out of the house. Now we shall have to talk about something more convincing: cooking first of all, then perhaps cats, and people, and politics. The news over the radio, I am sure, is as bad as ever.

Dialogue Two

MARCELINO

The other day, Don Rafael, you said you were. In no uncertain terms.

DON RAFAEL

So I was. And I am again. After a few days and a few intermittences, as a few nights of sleep appear to have been, it is very astonishing but quite so: I am.

MARCELINO

And almost exactly the same. How do you do it? But before we get to that question, if we ever do, I have another one. On more or less thinking it over I have about decided that if the terms in which you are were no uncertain ones, I at least am very uncertain about them. You make Being, or at least your being, a subjective act or event, and not an object—but that is as much as I seem to understand.

DON RAFAEL

My poor Marcelino, you have not understood that much. I am very willing to let Being be an object, indeed I want it to be, and my own being is largely an object, to myself as well as to you, but why restrict Being to being an object? It is also a subject. What is the difficulty? Can there still be an argument to the effect that if Being is objective, then subjectivity, as the opposite of objectivity, must also be an opposite of Being, that is, a sort of Not-Being? That is a piece of schematic sophistry that convinces nobody at this time of day. Even for Plato, Not-Being is a kind of Being. Assuming that it is, one can sophistically or logically say that even if the subjectivity were a kind of Not-Being it would also be a kind of Being.

MARCELINO

So you would say that the objective and the subjective are distinct kinds of being.

DON RAFAEL

Almost. They are not very distinct, since for example the subjectivity is always full of objects or versions of objects and it often functions more or less objectively, as in recognizing facts, in counting things arithmetically or in arranging them in logical patterns. And the subjectivity exists as an objective fact, as any exasperated politician can tell you. But if the subjectivity and objectivity are not clearly separate, and certainly not polar opposites, they are distinguishable, and I would say they are at least two different kinds of Being. Not opposite, not even necessarily complementary, like positive and negative, but anyhow different kinds of Being, and not the only kinds.

MARCELINO

I suppose not. I can think of several other kinds, at this rate, such as Potentiality, Material, Process, Force, Motion, Time, all those things which are often considered opposite to or rigidly distinct from Being. But are we going to include in Being, or among the kinds of Being, not only things that have been, or are, or will be, but things that never were or can be, everything that might have been or might be but will not? Are we going to include what never could have been, such as the conquest of Mexico by Emily Dickinson? Are we going to include everything imaginable and unimaginable in Being?

DON RAFAEL
Yes.

MARCELINO
It makes me dizzy.

DON RAFAEL
Because you never studied theology properly, as if it might have to be believed. The mind of God, being infinite, quite naturally includes all the kinds of Being you have mentioned and many more, and since they are all in His mind they necessarily are and possess to perfection their kind of Being.

MARCELINO
You mean that in the mind of God Emily Dickinson could have conquered Mexico?

DON RAFAEL
Not could have, she did. Or rather, under a certain kind of theology, since in His mind nothing is possible or past but all is actual, Miss Dickinson is at this moment in the act of conquering Mexico. Not only God, but I too, can see her now, more plainly in fact than I do you.

MARCELINO
I know that some of your best friends were Surrealists in your youth, but isn't it time to stop?

DON RAFAEL
No. I think it is time to begin again, high time. And all that is really needed is a reform of the Sunday Schools, to make them give more time to theology.

MARCELINO
But if everything indiscriminately and sense-lessly is in Being, it does seem to be, as Kant said it was, an empty concept.

DON RAFAEL

How can it be an empty concept when it includes everything? My master Ortega, who liked to have his little jokes, remarked that Kant suffered from ontophobia, an irrational terror of Being, especially of any concrete being. You suffer from ontophobia, too, but it is, in your case, a rational terror of irrational forms of Being. My poor Marcelino, you will never become a saint.

MARCELINO

Nor, I suppose, directly a philosopher. What a relief! But even so, let me courageously agree that everything that is or is not, to put it briefly, is included in Being, and as Being is thus the totality of absolutely everything, I suppose it is one. But, with all due respect, Don Rafael, you do not possess it or anything like it.

DON RAFAEL

Something very like it. Possessing all of Being is of course the privilege of God alone, though merely being in relation to it, distinct from it if not contrary to it, corresponding to it or being included in it does seem to make more of one's own being, one's little fraction of Being. But there is much more: not only is the bare fact that I exist final and actual; I also share in potentiality, both what I may still be and what I might or might not have been—say a world-famous painter or ballet dancer. What I actually am not, what I could have been and what I could not have been, are as much a part of what I am as the mere residual facts of what I have been and am now, as you see me, a blind man of flesh and bone who pays his taxes.

MARCELINO

This is more than a little like Don Quijote's feeling that he could have been Roland or all the paladins of Charlemagne in one, or Cortés, or, except for a sense of direction, one of the great saints.

DON RAFAEL

Exactly. And notice that objectively, in external fact, he was not all the paladins, but that subjectively, in internal fact, he was. He most abundantly was. So that the being of Don Quijote, truly and even objectively considered, *has* to include the paladins, though they were only partly realized in his overt adventures.

MARCELINO

But if the being or essence of Don Quijote includes the paladins, it also includes the overt facts, the residual facts, as you call them—which we are including in Being still, I trust—namely, the grotesque failures and a figure which is, to a surprising number of people, simply comic.

DON RAFAEL

Of course. Even the fact that many people mistakenly think he is a simple comic figure is part of the being of Don Quijote. But he is only one example of the paladins as a potential, an interior force, if you like. Sometimes they are more successful in overt performance. Cortés thought he was Roland or Amadis or whatever, and succeeded in behaving accordingly.

MARCELINO

But he had luck on his side. He was an amazingly high-handed thief. His only ideal was a title in the nobility back home.

DON RAFAEL

None of that interferes with the scale of his accomplishments. If he had been only objective, or honest, or devoted to a higher cause than a title, Mexico could never have been conquered.

MARCELINO

Should it have been?

DON RAFAEL

That is another question. You have the same thing today, for better or for worse, in de Gaulle, who has variously thought he was Joan of Arc, Napoleon, and Louis XIV. To the simple-minded realism of the Anglo-Saxon world he has been irritating and absurd, but in fact he has accomplished things on the scale of Joan of Arc, Napoleon, and Louis XIV, sometimes with as much treachery as Cortés and with as silly a notion of heraldic splendor. It is easily said that he has no business in history, he is an anachronism, but history is in fact made up largely of anachronisms.

MARCELINO

No doubt. During one of the Restorations Victor Hugo said that God seemed to have got mixed up as to which century it was.

DON RAFAEL

That is Hugo for you. He always tried to go too far and rarely went far enough. God is *always* mixed up as to which century, or which centuries, plural, it is. He may be actuality itself to the theologians but He is never on the side of pure contemporaneity.

MARCELINO

But, Don Rafael, if we are going to mean all that, all those kinds and dimensions and mixtures of things, by Being, I don't think the word will stand it. It will convey all that meaning to nobody but ourselves, and I may as well tell you I am going to lose track of what we are meaning by it any minute now.

DON RAFAEL

I too. But is there another word? I have been

thinking I might work up a technical noun out of the Spanish verb *hay*.

MARCELINO
There is? There are?

DON RAFAEL
Freely translated, yes. But *there* suggests a locality, like the *∂a* in *Dasein*. *Hay* would not commit us to either Existence or to ideal Being or anything else, not even here or there, time or eternity.

MARCELINO
Not to the present?

DON RAFAEL
I'm afraid it would. And I cannot think of a decent noun. *Hayi∂a∂? Hayia? Habersei∂a∂?* Much worse than *vivencia!* Ortega was better at this kind of game.

MARCELINO
How about Beingishness? That would leave everything open and not commit us to the present, to the objective or the subjective, or to local existence. We could include all that and everything else in the one word, Beingishness.

DON RAFAEL
You have bad ears, but consult them. You don't find that word repulsive?

MARCELINO
Not especially, but it is too plainly indefinite. And we are being definite.

DON RAFAEL
Not that we should be, but we are.

MARCELINO
Then how about Somethingness?

DON RAFAEL

Somethingness. Somethingness. *Algoiðað.* I think you have it.

MARCELINO

Etwasheit. Quelquechoséité. Tomorrow I shall start writing a reply to Sartre, entitled *L'Etre ou la Quelquechoséité!*

DON RAFAEL

Why not to Heidegger: *Etwas unð Ewigkeit?*

MARCELINO

We sound like a couple of retired professors.

DON RAFAEL

All too properly. But I think we are getting somewhere, which is not very becoming. Somethingness. I shall have to ponder over *algoiðað,* but Somethingness sounds almost like good English.

MARCELINO

At least it sounds as if it could include everything. There is a passage in Gertrude Stein to the effect that "anything is something," and that would go for objective phenomena, thoughts, numbers, impossibilities, and all. But now we have a great sea of somethingness, as Dante or Plato might say, and what of it? Do we navigate it? Is it charted?

DON RAFAEL

Ah, mostly uncharted, unsounded. Out of say the seven seas of Somethingness, only two or three are known in any detail. The physical sciences, though so restricted, are still quite vague, history is very scattered and piecemeal, and so on. Do you mind?

MARCELINO

No, I don't think I do. I certainly should not

34

like to know everything myself and I should not really like everything to be known. But what is the use of this Somethingness? Are we any better off with a great sea of Somethingness than we were with a great sea of Being, or the Great Chain, for that matter?

DON RAFAEL

Yes, we are better sustained. Most theories of Being, from Parmenides on, tend to set Being against something else, like Not-Being, or Time, or Material, or the Subjectivity, or Potentiality, and since most of our life goes on in the terms that are not those of Being we begin to feel we are in the main nonentities, or mere shadows of something more solid. This feeling of dissolution into Not-Being can be a source of *Angst* or anguish, terror, or whatever is in fashion now, and simple alienation from the universe, *Verworfenheit* and destitution, or being lost. Well, one can feel that way, and cultivate a sort of nausea or vertigo, but the point is that even the worst forms of alienation from Being are *something*, inescapably something and not nothing. Even if I had been dead for years, I would still be something. I would be the late Don Rafael, even if nobody referred to me as such or remembered me. I would be the forgotten Don Rafael, and that would be something. This really does make a difference in how you feel about the world and hence in how you see it and live and act in it. It radically changes what those remote cousins of ours call our *Lebenswelt*, the world as we live in it.

MARCELINO

I don't think I really mind, Don Rafael, but some of that change is only verbal. We wave a noun at everything and all of a sudden, as if by magic, everything becomes substantial. Just because Somethingness is a substantive. It does have an adjectival color, but even that

35

is not so true to the processiveness in the universe as the participial or gerundive color of the noun *Being*. At least it feels like a noun. Not that I mind, really, and the use of nouns is not so loose as that of numbers, but do you think either of us would have liked this idea of Somethingness, of being ineluctably something, when we were young?

DON RAFAEL

No. Not the way you are putting it. The young do not care to think they are already something. They like to think they are going to be something, and something substantial, but they would not care to be told that this prospective state, of going to be something, is already something. It sounds as if their present lives were already settled and finished, no matter how we refine the argument and say that freedom and inconclusiveness and indefinition and process are also something. I remember not liking even to be told I was young, since that seemed to be that, conclusively, as if I would never grow up. But at our age it is pleasant to say or be told we are inevitably something. It keeps us in the world. Now that we have retired from an active life, from the universities, and shall before very long retire from the living world, we could easily have a vertigo of nonentity if it were not that alive or dead we are still inevitably and indisputably something, and integral to the Somethingness of everything else. Bless the noun! Thank God for it! Of course we could interpret Being to much the same effect, but it would take forever extricating what we would mean by Being from what so many people, from Parmenides on, have variously meant by it.

MARCELINO

But, aside from inspiring a general feeling that we are solidly in the world, is this notion of Somethingness at all interesting? Taken by itself it can seem as

36

blank and featureless as Being, taken by itself.

DON RAFAEL

I should think it would be less interesting by itself even than Being by itself. If it is ever dealt with and systematized by a technician it should pose fewer problems and solve almost none. But interest, since you mention it, exists only for living creatures—people, animals, and perhaps plants—inside of Life, which is a very small and special sector of Somethingness. For all the absolute immensity and exhaustiveness of Somethingness its interest is extremely slight, especially since only you and I have ever heard of it and we have scarcely the beginning of a theory of it. Nevertheless, a sense of Somethingness, made more conscious by a theory of it, might easily heighten the interest of many more things, both existing and potential, in our *Lebenswelt* than a sense of Being trained by the typical theories of it.

MARCELINO

Perhaps many more things would be interesting, casual details, haphazard arrangements, imperfections, futilities, and so on, which the usual sense of Being ordinarily neglects, but would the interest be as intense, in things all equally something, as the interest in the things of Being heightened by a context of Not-Being? The things of Being have, as it were, a dramatic shadow or a black background against which they are the brighter and assert themselves the more.

DON RAFAEL

But we are not excluding Being and Not-Being in the least. They are both eminently something. If you need a vivid chiaroscuro as a ground of interest, I should say it is even improved under our theory, since the context of Not-Being becomes not nothing but a solidly negative something. Under the usual theories of Being, the attention neglects or hurries past or shrinks from the things of Not-Being. Quite as you, being a sort of rationalist and even a sort of practical man, pay too little attention to the irrational, to the imaginary, and to what you think is insignificant. There are philosophical advantages to being blind, since the visible world is to me imaginary, and the world of the imagination more vivid. Calderón said, only from the point of view of theology, that life is a dream; I say so from experience. He added that dreams too are dreams; I say so too, but now I also say they are something. Likewise, for our theory, I know with great intimacy millions of details of space, by touch and feeling, details of sound, by a more acute or attentive hearing, which are nothing at all to you but very adequately something to me.

MARCELINO

I should imagine, too, that, being relieved of the constant crowding company of visible objects, you have a clearer sense of being yourself something?

DON RAFAEL

Clearer, yes, but not at all new. One does not have to be blind to be aware of being distinctly something. The blind have a rather heightened solitude, and so are more distinctly something to themselves, but we are still very much among all the other somethings that exist, even if a great many of them have to be transposed to the mode of the imaginary. Insofar as they are then inside us, we know them better. But there are many other kinds of solitude and as many kinds of association with other somethingnesses and Somethingness itself. Some of the blind may feel out of things, *verworfene* and even lost, but not I, and the blind in general have a name for being remarkably cheerful.

38

MARCELINO

But cheer is not Spanish. You always told
me it is an animal flush in the Saxons.

DON RAFAEL

Alegria, then. The point is, if you will let me
make it, that we blind people are not left out but remain in
the midst of life and, I think, deeper in than you people
with sight, who have distances always before you.

MARCELINO

And life, you say, is a very small sector of
Somethingness, and a substantial dream. At that rate it is
not much. Why should you be so *alegre* at being deeper in
it than I am? What do you see in it?

DON RAFAEL

Obviously not what you do. My *videncia*, to
use Don Antonio's comic word in all seriousness, will not
be yours, though there will be a resemblance. It is a little
as if I were the director of a play, standing behind the
scenes, and you were in the audience. I have to imagine
how the show is going, and though you see it you may not
see what is in it. Nor may I, for that matter, since the
Author is Anonymous. Whatever His message may be, the
show of our *Lebenswelt* goes on, and since you began being
my disciple at the age of seventeen, I think I may call
myself the director properly enough. The show is not mine,
but it is my version of it.

MARCELINO

No objection. I like your being a director
instead of setting up, like Socrates, for a metaphorical
midwife.

DON RAFAEL

Well, the metaphor would not work in your

case. You are not pregnant with ideas. But I will say for you that you make a pretty good member of the audience, perhaps even a good reviewer.

MARCELINO

Good or not, I will no doubt give you a rave notice.

DON RAFAEL

Thank you, but you ought to mention that the director belongs to a particular school of directing. The Stanislavsky behind me would be an uneasy combination of Ortega and Unamuno, and behind them—

MARCELINO

Never mind, Don Rafael. It is this particular show that is interesting, and you are the director.

DON RAFAEL

This metaphor is going to break down at any minute, but while it still seems to cohere, let me add two observations. This is, in all our circumstances, a peripheral show, an off-Broadway venture with scant hopes of getting "on."

MARCELINO

Broadway would be the major current philosophies?

DON RAFAEL

That, but also any big time. Life and the times as the news weeklies and mass media can see them, or as God can see them. Roughly speaking, we are in private. But my other observation, which is more worth laboring, is that outside and beyond our theatre, outside our *Lebenswelt* with its present show going on, lies an infinity of Somethingness, not only the Broadway shows, but the nation and other nations, other planets, other suns, galaxies and so on. Very many of these outer somethingnesses are, these metaphorical ones like those in literal astronomy, most visible by night. But whether or not you see them, with your daylight mind, our life is as much something as all the rest of it. And our life is after all open to somethingness at large, and pervaded by a good deal of it.

MARCELINO
But in itself, is it something definite?

DON RAFAEL
Would you mind if it were?

MARCELINO
Not now.

DON RAFAEL
Some people like nothing better than making life out something definite. We Spanish especially. I had a teacher in Madrid, who later became a priest, and he said that Life was "a primary ontological entity, absolute and authentic." How does that sound to you?

MARCELINO
Flattering. I see how he might have been a priest, for whom Life would be an arbitrary gift of the Living God. But one is usually told that life is a contingent phenomenon in the physical world, an excessive development of biological organisms, themselves a deviation from the good behavior of crystals. In short, life is anything but a primary ontological entity.

DON RAFAEL
Be careful. As part of the history of the physical universe, life cannot, we think, be primary, not in the sense of first in time, or preliminary and fundamental to the universe. But that is not strictly ontology. For Morente, ontology, or the study of what things are, depended heavily

on theology, on the God who made things be, whereas now it tries to depend on the sciences, as if life and everything else were phenomena which have their definite being by virtue of processes in the physical universe.

MARCELINO
Well, what is wrong with that view?

DON RAFAEL
Nothing at all, except that you do not live as if you were simply a phenomenon in the physical universe, and it does not look much as if it could be done.

MARCELINO
But Don Rafael, we are a species of higher ape, we are composed largely of chemical process and biological process. We take our vitamins.

DON RAFAEL
I have no objections to being a chemical process or a species of ape. I take my vitamins and walk upright. Let us not lose track of our physical nature, since we are not aspiring to holy orders. But there is more to my life than my animal nature, and telling myself I am a biochemical something is no help whatever in trying to live. How does a biochemical something go about anything, even its basic animal needs? There is nothing to be said against the behavior of the higher and lower animals, perhaps, but in any case they are not convincing models of conduct.

MARCELINO
Well, we are a very special species.

DON RAFAEL
No doubt. Plato is supposed to have said man is a featherless biped. Which Diogenes made ridiculous by coming into the agora holding a plucked chicken and

announcing it as Plato's idea of man. No doubt Plato himself was ridiculing the notion of deriving an adequate definition of man from natural history.

MARCELINO

But it is said, more adequately, that man is a rational animal.

DON RAFAEL

No doubt. But do you live as a rational animal? Or do you know how a rational animal would live? Would it spend all its waking hours on Reason—on formal logic, mechanics, profitable work and scientific investigation, anything, so long as it is reasonable? And would it be reasonable? If one considers the brevity of life, is it reasonable to spend much of one's time on reason and exclusively rational things?

MARCELINO

No, but a little of one's time, surely.

DON RAFAEL

Of course. Reason is a sort of appetite that wants satisfaction, and varies from one constitution to another. But while we are attending to these commonplaces, there is an important one we should not overlook, the view that man is a political animal.

MARCELINO

Oh yes, we have lived under that one most of our lives.

DON RAFAEL

And most of it has been a waste of time.

MARCELINO

Has it, really? I know that in the thirties I fell into the habit of seeing the political bearings of anything

43

whatever, especially pieces of literature. I did not go so far as our Marxist fellow-travelers and see almost all literature as political, and all of Proust or Joyce as little tracts against bourgeois society. Still, I did think that people who claimed to be non-political, like Mann, were being evasive if not downright disgusting, and nothing was worse than the pretention to being above politics, the ivory tower and art for art's sake. How ridiculous I was!

Don Rafael

Well, were you? I too went in for condemning anything that was even remotely connected with Fascism, the whole culture of Germany, for instance, and almost all Italian and Japanese. And I was very tolerant of the most miserable Leftist literature. I took up Russian. But was I being ridiculous? Were we both? I don't think so. We did take the obvious political movements too easily as final standards of value, or trusted them too naively to embody exactly the values we assumed they represented, but I don't think we were at all mistaken about our values. They were not specifically political, though they were being vividly and often clumsily or dishonestly fought out in political and military terms.

Marcelino

Yes, it is strange. I see I was often ridiculous but on the other hand I have not really changed my mind. Under the politics things seem to me about as they were. Have we given up being political animals?

Don Rafael

No more than we have given up being featherless bipeds or rational animals. We have only learned that political causes do not really cover as much of the case as we thought, the case of the arts or the case of our lives. Politicians and theorists of the Communist cause or the Capitalist cause would of course like to have us feel that

44

the value of everything, the meaning of our lives and the actual living of them, is ultimately their affair and subject to them, but it is not so. They do enter our lives, not only by controlling our money to a large extent but also by forcing themselves on our attention and occupying our minds for at least a few hours a day. They have great difficulty making themselves interesting, and they insist extravagantly, as if their very existence depended on our giving them a little attention each day, like house plants to be watered. But that is their problem, not ours. We pay them a polite amount of attention and in any case we do not try to cut our lives off from politics entirely, nor from reason or biological functions. Our life includes all that.

MARCELINO
But we are not independent of those conditions or above them.

DON RAFAEL
No. I think Morente would have liked us to be, as absolute ontological entities, even if he could not quite say we were. No, we are not independent. The most we can call ourselves is insubordinate.

MARCELINO
That is already a good deal.

DON RAFAEL
Perhaps not enough, after all. Seen from the inside, from the acting side of almost anything we do, it does look and feel as if our actions were ultimately arbitrary, done in freedom of choice. In retrospect we or anybody else can see our action as a mechanical and inevitable functioning of motives derived mainly, in my case, from an agrarian aristocracy and professional class in Spain, and in your case, from belated pioneers and a rising middle class in America. On reflection we have been behaving and

thinking exactly like rather international bourgeois intellectuals serving not so much our own interests as those of our class in this particular phase of its history. But in the prospect or course of any action, if we consulted the interests of the middle class, which in fact we never do, what advice could we possibly get, and would we take it? As classes go, the middle class is a pretty good one, but one spends remarkably little time serving its interests. Less than we spend on our biochemical interests and the rest. Within our livingness we may call our souls our own.

MARCELINO
Our what?

DON RAFAEL
Our souls. You cannot misunderstand what I mean by the word now, can you? I do not call the soul immortal or derive it from God necessarily, as Morente would, but that is no reason for denying its existence, and there is no better word for what I mean. Consciousness is too restricted, mind is too static, too much a matter of understanding or of philosophy, and reason or intellect do not convey enough of the notion of living. Soul. *Alma*. The words may be disreputable but they are quite exact. And I will even use the word spirit. For certain kinds of livingness it is indispensable.

MARCELINO
You would oblige me very much, Don Rafael, if you gave me a manifestation, a nice, comfortable, concrete, self-evident instance.

DON RAFAEL
Nothing could be simpler. In Spanish at least we know exactly what we mean when we say a bullfighter has soul, or that he has not. Let us say he has, to begin with, bravery, elegance, and a distinct personal style. All that is

difficult and precious enough, but it is simply character, not soul. Perhaps you might call it expression. Soul is the actual force that commands the expression and the character in performance, uses them as its instruments.

MARCELINO

Good. We have the same thing, or the plain and painful lack of it, in pianists, in dancers, in actors.

DON RAFAEL

Not only in the arts. It is evident often enough in the way a person walks, or laughs, or says a word, in any expression.

MARCELINO

Could it be called personality?

DON RAFAEL

No. Personality is a matter of specific character, one of the instruments of the soul. But the confusion is common, especially among actors, plainly among comedians. But if the actor is confused, elaborating a personality without a soul, the audience is not. Any commonplace actor can make with a personality, and that is entertaining enough, but the star actor is the one with a soul, probably unaware of it, or at best resigned to it as a mysterious something he cannot really control. He can make very careful allowances for it, prepare for it, and so on, but his attention had better not be on it.

MARCELINO

Yes, better not. Nothing is worse than somebody being soulful.

DON RAFAEL

It must have been all the people being soulful, the sub-Romantics with their *schöne Seelen* as much as inanely religious people who gave the soul a bad name.

47

Nevertheless, even under another name or with no name at all, its presence or absence in any performance is perfectly evident to any witness or audience. The witness may not be articulate about what he feels or recognizes, he may simply exclaim or yell or rise to his feet, but that is nothing against the existence of an actual manifestation of soul, even philosophically speaking.

MARCELINO
And biochemically? Politically?

DON RAFAEL
No doubt it is some mutation of energy, a phosphorescence. In politics it is especially powerful, and very dangerous. In great leaders, like Hitler, or de Gaulle, or Kennedy, you get a mystique or a charisma which may be good or evil, depending. There are very evil souls. It is too bad we no longer believe in demons and possession; they made certain things much clearer. But political leaders are another problem.

MARCELINO
And terrible. Especially if you do not like being led.

DON RAFAEL
Well, we have mentioned them. We have done our duty by them.

MARCELINO
Don Rafael, our good behavior all round is extraordinary. We have even been serious about the soul. We deserve a drink.

Dialogue Three

MARCELINO
Schelling says something very interesting.

DON RAFAEL
You don't say!

MARCELINO
I'm afraid I do. If I had been reading Schelling it might not be so interesting, but I found it quoted in a Spanish book, and somehow it is very interesting, as if it were Spanish or even Moorish.

DON RAFAEL
Moorish?

MARCELINO
Well, so it strikes me. He says that certain crystals have hexagonal souls.

DON RAFAEL
Very pretty. It may not be very Moorish, but it is very pretty indeed.

MARCELINO
If I had read it in Schelling I would have said yes, of course, he has been reading Novalis, who was very mystic about minerals and the soulfulest German who ever came along. But turning up in a Spanish book all by itself, without the context of German Romanticism to compromise it, it is a very interesting little thing.

DON RAFAEL

It makes a nice problem. Do hexagonal crystals have hexagonal souls? One could very well say that such crystals acquire their hexagonal expressions by virtue of a hexagonizing force. The force may not itself be hexagonal but at least it hexagonizes, and one could quite well call that force the soul of the crystal.

MARCELINO

Well, at least Schelling did, and I suppose Novalis genuinely felt that among crystals he was in company, among fellow souls though he was not himself hexagonal, to my knowledge.

DON RAFAEL

No, but he was an assessor of salt mines. That makes a useful difference: he lived or made a living by evaluating quantities of salt, but his livingness was a communion with an innumerable host of tiny crystal souls.

MARCELINO

I think he was simply a nitwit.

DON RAFAEL

Because you do not happen to be a mystical pantheist. But regardless of what you think you know about hexagons and crystals in a scientific way, that peculiar *vivencia* of Novalis is something, and something with more livingness to it than his assessments.

MARCELINO

Or his command of geology. But I mentioned those unlikely souls in crystals by way of asking you how far livingness can go. I should think it would be limited to organic life, to plants and animals and man, but here is Schelling extending it to minerals and geometry.

DON RAFAEL

We have got to distinguish again between life

50

and livingness, between the real and the imaginary, and a number of other confusions. In the old days I would have gone to the blackboard to mark it all out, but let me see whether I can put some of it in order by talking.

MARCELINO

Perhaps I can draw a little plan of what you say. I really have to see things.

DON RAFAEL

It is a limitation. Much of this will not be spatial, but do as you please. Let us begin with where we are and what we have, with the soul. We do not call it a state of consciousness or an awareness of presences now, but just the soul until further notice.

MARCELINO

Good. I will make it round, not hexagonal.

DON RAFAEL

I suppose that is an improvement, but try to remember that as a force it really has no shape of its own. We may say it is alive.

MARCELINO

Fine. And what does it do?

DON RAFAEL

It likes excitement and it likes repose.

MARCELINO

I suppose it does, about equally. Why does it like them?

DON RAFAEL

I haven't the remotest idea. But it likes them. And it likes to be concentrated and it likes to be diffuse.

MARCELINO

How about objects?

DON RAFAEL

Of course it likes objects. And it likes a change of objects. It likes to be with objects and it likes to be away from them.

MARCELINO

But if it is away from objects it goes to sleep.

DON RAFAEL

It likes to sleep.

MARCELINO

Oh.

DON RAFAEL

But when it is not asleep it likes to have something going on. Whatever it is may be going on very slowly and quietly or very fast and violently and the soul may or may not like the pace and the intensity just then, but it does like something to be going on. When things outside it are standing quite still then the soul does the going on, often at a very slow pace, but it does go on and does not stop except to sleep.

MARCELINO

Would you say the soul is a process in time?

DON RAFAEL

No. That would be true but not true enough. The soul stays pretty well where it is, it does not really get anywhere, so we had better not call it a process; and we are not speaking now of objective or historical time but of an internal change or variability, a sort of motion. I am trying to speak of the soul as distinct from its objects, and that is not easy.

MARCELINO

Then I had better not disturb you.

DON RAFAEL

Not just now. Just listen a moment. The question is what the soul wants of objects when it is liking to be with them. As the soul varies, it will want various qualities and various arrangements of its objects from time to time, and the most troublesome difference in the qualities of objects is that some are alive and variable like the soul, some are invariable, and some are variable but not alive. The soul variously likes to be with all these kinds of things, but what does it want of them, and what does it want of each kind?

MARCELINO

You are not asking *me* that question?

DON RAFAEL

No. But I only have part of an answer. What the soul wants of most of its objects is the pleasure of their company.

MARCELINO

Whether or not it gets any such pleasure?

DON RAFAEL

Of course. There are all sorts of things to be done in the company of animate and inanimate objects, warfare, seduction, games, and just sitting around. Any of it may turn out painful but the company is sought by the soul for some pleasure or other in it. But there are numberless objects whose company the soul does not seek. Some the soul treats as strangers or as servants, and some perfectly companionable objects it snubs. It could all be very complicated, and instead of opening into a sociology or a social register of the soul and its objects, let me try to be clear on one relation, that of the soul to a hexagonal crystal.

MARCELINO

A crystal with a soul of its own?

53

DON RAFAEL

Not just now. Let us begin with a hexagonal crystal quietly sitting there in a clear steady light. Now the human soul perceives that crystal. What do we get?

MARCELINO

A perception.

DON RAFAEL

That is very diplomatic of you. You take a neutral ground. But from subjective ground, from the point of view of the soul, and not simply from that of the optical mechanism, the perception is an experience.

MARCELINO

An *Erlebnis*.

DON RAFAEL

Yes. Or what I think Ortega meant by *vivencia*. It is more than bare perception; it involves a good many dispositions or more or less faint responses in the soul toward brightness, symmetry, stillness, a bulk wider than its base, and so on. The perception is a relatively simple affair and almost objective; the experience, as something lived through by the soul, can be extraordinarily complex and largely vague or inarticulate.

MARCELINO

But nevertheless something.

DON RAFAEL

Its reality is not in question. Nor its unmanageable complexity, especially when you consider that the experience, the *vivencia*, will vary immensely according to the sensitivity and resources of response from one human soul to another.

MARCELINO

Which brings up the question of communication.

54

DON RAFAEL

No. Not now. Let us now suppose that somebody is moving the crystal about in the light, and it is made to utter its limited vocabulary of glowing, gleaming, glittering, glimmering, flashing, shining, some of these simultaneously from the several edges and surfaces, and let us say at uneven intervals and not simply in rotation. It now has a vivacity.

MARCELINO

Oh, my God! You are saying it is alive!

DON RAFAEL

No. It is tempting to say so, and you seem to feel the temptation, as I do, but I resist. No. Our crystal is being lively but not alive. *Lebendig* if you like. Let us be careful and note that an inanimate thing as well as a live thing, like the soul, can be lively, and that liveliness is often a common property as it were, a sort of viability in the association of a soul and a crystal.

MARCELINO

Then how about livingness?

DON RAFAEL

We are clearing the ground for that, but first let me make sure we are not forgetting something in all the excitement of our lively crystal. Our first crystal, inert and with no variety of light, can be quite as good a companion for the soul when it is having a liking for repose. We may want the second crystal to calm down and stop its nonsense, to affect in our presence no more than the mere hexagonal lucidity which is its true and essential character. If it does behave itself, in a properly unanimated way, the livingness of our association with it can be as great as that of our association with the lively crystal. It comes down to this: the degree of liveliness is no measure of the degree of livingness.

55

MARCELINO
Obviously.

DON RAFAEL
Not obviously at all. In this age which is obsessed with liveliness, with supersonic speeds, racing, explosions, with everything in its cinematic aspect, how can it be obvious that livingness, or simply life, can exist to the same degree in quietude?

MARCELINO
Well, the passivities and quiescences and vegetations of the East have come into vogue. Has flower power come to your attention?

DON RAFAEL
Yes. If it makes what I said obvious, so much the better. But I am speaking in a much more general way.

MARCELINO
And you were not excluding liveliness from livingness but including it in livingness along with repose.

DON RAFAEL
Yes. And to proceed: if livingness belongs, as I think we shall find it does, to the soul, both liveliness and repose are properties common to the soul and its objects alike.

MARCELINO
Whether the objects are alive or not.

DON RAFAEL
Yes. But we still have not defined livingness, a term we have been using rather like an x in algebra. We cannot equate it with the soul.

MARCELINO
Why not?

DON RAFAEL

Because the soul, aside from going to sleep, can disappear, to itself, can "lose" itself, in its objects, in its preoccupations, in work, even in living. Shelley—not Schelling—

MARCELINO

I heard you, Don Rafael.

DON RAFAEL

You have such bad ears. Shelley, then, remarked that in living we lose the sense of life. I would say we lose the sense of livingness. Not necessarily, but we often do.

MARCELINO

Why not necessarily?

DON RAFAEL

I do not know why not, but the fact is that you can have a sense of livingness and live at the same time. That is what war dances and sports are for, at least in part, and of course I am going to say that that is what a great deal of art is for. Whatever the savage may think he is doing, accumulating mana or inwardly arming himself or binding the real process and outcome of the battle in advance, he is also abstracting the livingness of the battle from the battle. He will realize in his war dance the livingness of battle more clearly than he will in the battle itself.

MARCELINO

The livingness will not, I assure you, entirely disappear in battle. The battle will often look and feel to him exactly like a war dance. I speak from my own experience as a modern and university-trained savage, but I imagine it is generally true, that inside the battle itself the performance is appreciably a performance, theatrical as well as choreographed, and one is often both participant and witness, or spectator. And there is this dreary fact, that for many veterans the only real livingness in their lives was on the battlefield, whether they got medals for it or not.

DON RAFAEL

Well yes, one has to accept war, in part at least, as a form of art, which tries to isolate livingness. As our bullfighting does. That is the great human use of danger and sudden death, that it clarifies or isolates livingness, which paradoxically can seem more precious than life. And in passing let me say that eroticism has a lot to do with it; one speaks of courting danger and death, but it is the factor of heightened livingness that is in fact being courted.

MARCELINO

It seems an extreme case. Does livingness in general have to go on at that pitch?

DON RAFAEL

We have said it does not, when we put livingness in both liveliness and repose. Taking one's life in one's hands is something beyond liveliness and I am not sure it simplifies our question. But at this extreme a few things about livingness become clear which may or may not hold for milder manifestations. One thing is an actuality so intense that duration is a matter of moments. The person whose life is immediately at stake hardly reckons with a past and future beyond say an hour or a day. With the suspension of most of the past goes most of the personal history and even the personality of the person. Livingness involves a living person well enough or has to take place in him, but it is very nearly impersonal in a case like this one. The person obviously must have his capacities and habits

58

of long standing, but now they exist only as presently available and contribute to what is felt as essentially an improvisation. This quality of spontaneity, novelty, freshness, discovery, must, I think, exist in some degree in all livingness, no matter how ancient or habitual or familiar the materials, the circumstances, or even the attendant forms may be.

MARCELINO

As in a bullfight or a battle.

DON RAFAEL

Yes. In those extreme cases everything is traditional, conventional, known in advance, but each least motion is a novelty, as if it came from nowhere. Another strange thing occurs. When the torero or the soldier, supposing he survives, comes out of the action and returns to his full biographical self, his everyday self as it were, that self is a novelty. It is rediscovered and not discovered if you insist, but it is curiously unfamiliar and a surprise.

MARCELINO

It is very amusing.

DON RAFAEL

Of course. It can even amuse the person returning to himself. And this kind of absurdity is the staple of comedy and irony. At any rate it is one of the many locales of livingness. But if you ask the question whether the livingness in the bull ring or battlefield is greater than the livingness of the return of the torero or the soldier to himself, I have no answer. We have said the degree of liveliness does not measure the degree of livingness and I am inclined to agree with what we said. An adagio pastoral passage can be just as moving as an allegro passage.

MARCELINO
It can be deeper.

DON RAFAEL
Let us make no virtue of depth. Depth is for
Germans. We can accept profundity but we need not
prefer it. Your Greeks were very superficial.

MARCELINO
As Nietzsche said. What surfaces!

DON RAFAEL
We are being very careful not to define
livingness.

MARCELINO
Let me try a classic definition. Shall we start
off by assuming that livingness is a kind of experience?

DON RAFAEL
No. It would be a false start. Any experience,
all experience, in the sense of *Erlebnis* or *vivencia* has a
livingness of some kind. It can be quiet or lively or exalted,
and we may prefer the higher intensities of it, but in any
experience whatever there is a livingness. There is even a
livingness to boredom.

MARCELINO
In that case could we say that livingness is the
essence of experience?

DON RAFAEL
That sounds more promising. Please go on.

MARCELINO
Let me add that it is an activity of the soul,
which we may call its substance, and then go on to
distinguishing its matter, which would no doubt be the
objects of experience.

60

DON RAFAEL

Before we do go on, let us dwell a moment on your word activity. I agree to it, so long as it is not confined to action but includes also reaction to things or events from outside the soul, and even the maintaining of apathy in the face of outer events. If the willed stillness of the soul, as in so much of our Spanish Stoicism, from Seneca onwards—

MARCELINO

And in Greek Stoicism, where it is called *ataraxia*—

DON RAFAEL

If you are going to call such perfect stillness, aspired to by the Stoic soul if seldom attained, also an activity, then I will accept your term activity for all experiences. If there is no action, no reaction, not even a positive refusal to react, not even simple absorption, then, I take it, there is no experience. We suspend the question of what value we set on greater or lesser activity. The mere inert reflection of things by a mirror or a camera is not a livingness, but if assumed as a function, as with objective artists like Velasquez or Courbet, or reporters or scientists, it is an activity of the soul and a rather exciting one. All told, I think you are right.

MARCELINO

I think we had better say also that the livingness is ordinarily not conscious. One's attention is normally directed at objects, preoccupied with them, as if they existed in themselves without our experience of them. They have to be extremely painful or extremely pleasurable to distract our attention from themselves to our feelings about them.

DON RAFAEL

That is probably less true in the case of

women, who do think a great deal about their feelings and usually of objects only as they affect their feelings, but even so, yes, I think it is true that the attention of everybody is more on the objects of experience than on experience, or feelings about objects, or activities of the soul. So that we might say that the greater part of our life, in the sense of living, or of livingness, in your sense of the activity of the soul, goes on behind our backs.

MARCELINO
Our living then is largely inadvertent. Is that a mistake on our part, do you think?

DON RAFAEL
I don't know. It would be very tiresome to be thinking always of how one feels, of what one's livingness is just now, but all the same one does want to be in possession of one's life, to realize one's self living, and this cannot be done properly with one's mind constantly on objects.

MARCELINO
Not even when the objects are alive?

DON RAFAEL
Not even, perhaps even less. Living things are to most of us more preoccupying than inanimate objects, no matter how lively.

MARCELINO
So, to present livingness to ourselves, more or less extricated from its objects if not perfectly isolated, so we can realize and possess it, we get the war dance, sports, and the arts?

DON RAFAEL
Yes, those forms of activity may have other purposes, serving practical ends like successful warfare, physical fitness, and social propaganda of various kinds,

but what most interests us is their realization of livingness more distinctly than in practical activity.

MARCELINO

So we are agreed about that, the possession or realization of livingness is what most interests us in the arts, but does it interest more than a few other people who think vaguely as we do?

DON RAFAEL

Probably a great many people, whether or not they theorize about it as we do. Many want from the arts other things than we do, and many want from other things what we want from the arts, but an appetite for the possession of livingness in one way or another must be about as general as sexuality; one might as well include sexuality in it.

MARCELINO

And religion, wouldn't you say? They do talk about eternal life and the life everlasting, which is not reasonably imagined but is often very acutely felt, especially at the elevation of the Host and on taking communion, as the bread of life. The feeling is certainly one of possessing a vivid and complete livingness, whatever strange notions one may have of eternity.

DON RAFAEL

I think we could interpret a great majority of human motives as a desire for the possession of livingness. Feasts and holidays traditionally provide for it, not simply for rest from labor, and even a great deal of what is called serious activity or downright work contains a certain amount of it. The intense pleasure a craftsman or mechanic quite commonly gets from the shape and quality of his tools, and especially from the pace and adroitness of their handling—all distinct enough from the objective job to be done and the living to be made—is a realization of livingness.

MARCELINO
There is a lot of poetry in antiquity about that kind of thing that took me a long time to adjust to. There is a poem by Alcaeus about an armory, not a promising subject, unless you imagine the feeling of a warrior about his weapons, and it takes some time to realize that the poetry of the Georgics is not so much in the scenery or the beauties of Nature as it is in the work on the farm, much of it hard and even futile.

DON RAFAEL
There is no end to the instances, but they seem to me to make it clear that what we are dealing with in our word livingness is more than a verbal refinement on Ortega. We are not talking about an *Erlebnis* or an Experience, or a *vivencia* in that sense, which still conveys the objects or materials of living more than the essence of living or at least does not distinguish it and insist on it enough.

MARCELINO
Are we talking about esthetics any longer?

DON RAFAEL
Were we talking about them at all? I thought I got rid of them when I headed you off from defining livingness as a kind of experience instead of the essence of experience.

MARCELINO
Why do you mind esthetics? Why do I? Even the estheticians mind them, and certainly the artists do. But why is that?

DON RAFAEL
I do not speak for everyone, so far as I know,

but I have the same hatred of talk about esthetics as I have of talk about Life. Antonio Machado remarked that as soon as the cry goes up "One must live!" or "We must live!" you can be sure that people are getting ready to kill each other in vast numbers. And when private persons, young or old or at the dangerous age, talk about living their lives or being allowed to grow, you can be sure they are preparing to do something abominable. And when anybody announces he has a right to express himself you can be sure the self he expresses will be that of an animal. When somebody starts in on esthetics you have to be prepared for some claims to an experience so rarefied and a sensibility so exquisite that only God and His angels are worthy of it.

MARCELINO

Yes, one has to be prepared for that, but sometimes one is pleasantly surprised.

DON RAFAEL

Not often. More often there is an unpleasant surprise, which even Tolstoi provided, that art must be all within the competence of the peasantry or the masses. We get art reserved either for an elite or for the downtrodden, an elite in reverse, and this I hate.

MARCELINO

You take the arts that seriously? I suppose I should. At least I agree that the arts ought to be as indifferent to class as science is, or money, or religion. It should be for anybody.

DON RAFAEL

Perhaps it should mean to be for anybody. But whatever the audience, and whatever else the audience may want of it, art has something to do with livingness.

MARCELINO

All art?

DON RAFAEL

Certainly not. Not even all masterpieces, but for us all the most interesting art has something to do with livingness, and I would say the best art has the most to do with it.

MARCELINO

I may have my reservations, but for the moment I can't think what they are.

DON RAFAEL

Good. I shall run up a little classical scheme for you, in which you will feel at home. Temporarily.

MARCELINO

Not a monument but a motel of intellect?

DON RAFAEL

Why not? Let us say that the single universal substance is Somethingness, just for a foundation.

MARCELINO

We have said so.

DON RAFAEL

And life is a species of Somethingness?

MARCELINO

What else can it be?

DON RAFAEL

Well, it might be the essence of Somethingness, but we think it is not. We are not going to take on Spinoza and Leibniz and various mystics just now. We put them aside with Novalis.

MARCELINO

So life is a species of Somethingness. Now I know.

66

DON RAFAEL
And the soul is a species of life?

MARCELINO
And not the essence. Yes.

DON RAFAEL
We were saying that the soul is the substance
of experience, whatever the forms and objects, and that
the essence of experience is not the soul itself perhaps but
certainly an activity of the soul. And the actuality of that
activity we called livingness.

MARCELINO
And there we are.

DON RAFAEL
Approximately. But it is the next step that
bothers me. I am about to say that livingness, which is the
essence of any and all experience, is in the case of the arts,
also the substance. As the substance of artistic activity it
replaces the soul, or displaces it, or certainly crowds it
very seriously.

MARCELINO
You have lost me.

DON RAFAEL
Again you are short of theology. With a grasp
of transubstantiation you would have less difficulty. But
in your own terms—who is doing the singing in the *Iliad*?
Homer or the Muse?

MARCELINO
The Muse is told to do it, so I suppose she
does.

DON RAFAEL
And she is a goddess, a substantial and

constant livingness which has replaced the merely human soul, the fitful livingness in the old blind wandering bard. You may call her a figure of speech, but like such words as possession and inspiration, she indicates something perfectly real. In the same person, is the soul that sings recognizably the same soul as the one that speaks? The one that dances the same as the one that walks? The one that writes poetry the same as the one that writes prose?

MARCELINO

I would say no. But anyone might say yes, it is the same soul in a greater state of excitement, dealing with other objects and engaged in a different kind of activity.

DON RAFAEL

Then how can anyone tell it is the same soul? You might as well call a soul asleep and dreaming the same as the soul of the waking person. Anyhow, I think we are better off with transubstantiation.

MARCELINO

But why do we have to call it a different soul?

DON RAFAEL

Because for all practical purposes it is. There is a volume of Flaubert's letters on the table, with a slip of paper to mark a page, if Isabel did as I asked her to when she was reading to me. It is a sacred text, a wonderful passage. It begins, "C'est une chose délicieuse . . . "

MARCELINO

I have it. "C'est une chose délicieuse que d'écrire, que de ne plus être soi . . . "

DON RAFAEL

You see. He is no longer himself, and what he is now is not even a writer, but writing, an activity.

MARCELINO

" . . . mais de circuler dans toute la création
dont on parle . . . "

DON RAFAEL

How exact he is! His function is not a creation
nor to represent a part of Creation—that was perhaps
good enough for Zola—but to move around in it like a
living thing. We could say, like livingness. Go on. He gets
even more precise.

MARCELINO

"Aujourd'hui par exemple, homme et femme
tout ensemble, amant et maîtresse à la fois, je me suis
promené à cheval dans une forêt par une après-midi
d'automne sous les feuilles jaunes, et j'étais les chevaux, les
feuilles, le vent, les paroles qu'on se disait et le soleil rouge
qui faisait s'entrefermer leurs paupières noyées d'amour."

DON RAFAEL

It is all there! Notice that the horseback ride
is an experience of Emma Bovary and Rodolphe, rather
two very different erotic experiences. There we have
Erlebnis, *vivencia*. But the livingness is in the feelings of
Flaubert—and of the reader. It permeates everything in
the scene—circulates through the creation, as he says—
and goes well beyond a participation in the experience of
Emma and Rodolphe, it participates as well in the horses,
the yellow leaves, the red sunlight, and—Flaubert being
Flaubert—the very *words* the two lovers speak to each
other. He says that he *was* all those things, and notice that
many of them are inanimate things. The substantial
livingness pervading everything includes them.

MARCELINO

It sounds a little like God immanent in His
universe.

DON RAFAEL

You are coming along very nicely. It is indeed like the God of some theologies, certainly like the Holy Ghost in this case, who tends to circulate more than the other persons.

MARCELINO

Would pantheism make a good analogy?

DON RAFAEL

A good analogy to what I would call an artistic heresy. Let us, between ourselves, call the substantial livingness permeating a work of art the Muse. It is possible and even common to think that in a perfect work of art there should be nothing but the Muse, and then the work would indeed be a kind of pantheism in little.

MARCELINO

There is another kind of pantheism about works of art, that whatever happens to get into a work of art, by chance, incompetence, or simple spontaneity is, necessarily, all Muse.

DON RAFAEL

We cannot attend to all the latest heresies at once, even with a Vatican council. Let us return to the older heresy, that the work of art should have nothing in it but Muse, not that it automatically has. I mean the theory of pure art, or pure poetry, as Mallarmé and for that matter Flaubert sometimes aspired to make it. Flaubert wanted to write a book that would sustain itself on style alone and be *about* nothing. It is perhaps a beautiful aspiration, and in such a materially glutted age as the nineteenth century, that aspiration did at least help put subject matter in its place. But the theory is at best a vanishing point and cannot be realized. In the book or the poem most thoroughly saturated with style at its most intense or dazzling, there are still the old tribal words, the inert material, which the Muse in the work cannot invent and must remain objects to her. In art there is a dualism which simply cannot be transcended, however hard the best people try. One can give "a purer sense" to the tribal words, manipulate them, juggle them, even distort and crossbreed them as Joyce did, but the brute material words remain. And they get us into trouble with the analogy of more orthodox theology, since they are not mere material, they have a form of their own, which does not proceed from the Muse in the "creation," though she may indeed alter it very considerably.

MARCELINO
She animates it.

DON RAFAEL
Yes, exactly. Even more exactly, she permeates it with livingness, which we have said need not be lively.

MARCELINO
Since we are talking about literature, could we say that rhetoric is a liveliness of words, which livingness can use or leave alone, and which can exist without livingness?

DON RAFAEL
Yes. The idea is not new but it does fit into our terms.

MARCELINO
I have an admission that may be new. I like rhetoric just by itself, when it is perfectly frigid and artificial and has nothing to do with livingness, so far as I can tell. I naturally like it when the Greeks indulge in it, a lot of Pindar, but I also like the worst of Góngora and Calderón.

DON RAFAEL

I imagine you even like Dante.

MARCELINO

Once in a while, yes. Even the terrible clutter of symbols and the footnotes about them. But what I think I am saying is that I can get along very nicely without livingness in my literature. It need not even be lively. I like a nice quiet objective form that minds its own business and does not agitate me or even know I am there.

DON RAFAEL

As a Classicist you are bound to like such things, and even confuse them with Being.

MARCELINO

You will admit they are something.

DON RAFAEL

I will even give them a value. They are exteresting.

MARCELINO

They are what?

DON RAFAEL

Exteresting. It is a word I invented when I was young, but it is very useful. Many works of art, and great ones if not really the greatest, keep you severely exterior to themselves, forbid your participation in any inwardness they may have, and leave you in the presence of a more or less fine surface of themselves as objects. They are like the crystals we were talking about, still or in motion. One cannot call them uninteresting. Nor again interesting, since they are really none of our business and do not involve us.

MARCELINO

I think you are committing philology, or etymology.

DON RAFAEL

Yes. Not that it settles anything or should determine usage but *interest* seems to mean in Latin an interinvolvement or a concern of one thing to another. I force it a little in meaning by it more distinctly an inward or vital concern. So I had to invent the word exteresting, to mean the perfectly valid relationship between the subjectivity and the impermeable unliving outside of an object. Uninteresting would refer to things with which one has no relation at all, or not a distinct one. And we must pay our profoundest respect to the category of the Uninteresting, because it is enormously the largest part of Somethingness.

MARCELINO

But in case of something exteresting, what happens to one's own livingness?

DON RAFAEL

Ah, there is a slight difficulty. Our livingness may be heightened, to a degree below the interesting but heightened nevertheless. There is nothing more exteresting than decoration, unless it is background music, but if you are out to dinner with a woman in a fancy restaurant there is no doubt at all that the decoration and the background music heighten your evening.

MARCELINO

A friend of mine who composes tells me that the incredible success of Musak is that never in his life has it made him listen.

DON RAFAEL

Precisely. In our scene at the restaurant one does not want to be distracted from the woman and the food and the wine by interesting music or by interesting wallpaper. But they should not be uninteresting either.

MARCELINO

But there are many exteresting things one can put one's mind directly on and keep it there.

DON RAFAEL

Very many. There must be as many degrees of the exteresting as there are of the interesting and the uninteresting, and many cases must be hard to distinguish, or futile, but in a general way I should say that the exteresting is a relation between the livingness of a subjectivity and an object without livingness.

MARCELINO

Which may heighten the livingness of the subjectivity to itself?

DON RAFAEL

Yes. I once used the word exteresting in a very pejorative way, as we thought Fancy very inferior to Imagination, Decoration to Art, or the Circus to the Drama, and so on. Even Calderón to Shakespeare. But these days, if I still think the Exteresting and the rest inferior to the Interesting and the rest, I think them not much inferior, and there are times when I would much prefer the company of objects, the Exteresting, to that of people or things bristling with a livingness of their own. One has an instinct for solitude as much as an instinct for gregariousness, and the livingness of solitude is heightened by objects, distracted and lessened by the untimely presence of other livingnesses.

MARCELINO

But if they are timely they are Interesting?

DON RAFAEL

Enormously. And we move from the subjectivity of solitude, or the objectivities of solitude, into the intersubjective.

MARCELINO
Naturally.

DON RAFAEL
Or artificially. In the most interesting kind of art, intersubjectivity is where we arrange to be.

MARCELINO
And in the least interesting philosophy. When reason and intuition both fail, then you can make do by putting two intuitions together and call it an intersubjective proof, supposing they agree.

DON RAFAEL
Yes, in philosophy it is a makeshift, in the arts it is primary, and it is too bad that philosophy or science sets the tone. One cannot help thinking that objectivity is where everything should be, that subjectivity is a failure of objectivity, and that intersubjectivity is a failure of both. Which puts the highest art in a very sad case, so sad that secondary art often tries to pretend it is objective to preserve its dignity, or in revolt it tries to be at least purely subjective. Subjectivity after all can be tolerated and can even assert its rights, as if they were those of the individual in politics. But nobody has a really kind word for inter-subjectivity.

MARCELINO
Shall we speak up for it?

DON RAFAEL
We must. But even between ourselves we must do more than assert its importance. We can say that in the arts it is more important than either objectivity or subjectivity. But then what? We had trouble enough a few days ago trying to disengage objectivity from subjectivity, and we will not have much better luck trying to disengage intersubjectivity from them both. It might be simpler if

intersubjectivity were only a plurality of subjectivities in accord or disaccord about something objective, but we have already introduced the transubstantiation of the livingness of the subject into that of the Muse and we may get the transformation of the objects of experience into symbols, by virtue of the livingness of intersubjectivity. Holy Communion itself is rudimentary compared to the full category of the Intersubjective.

MARCELINO
Perhaps we should let it go until Sunday.

Dialogue Four

MARCELINO
The day is clear and blue and the mountains have so much being in them they hurt.

DON RAFAEL
They are red, are they not?

MARCELINO
Reasonably red. A dull reddish, but red.

DON RAFAEL
A sort of sienna?

MARCELINO
You might say so.

DON RAFAEL
I remember them redder, close to lacquer.

MARCELINO
I do not see it. Not today.

DON RAFAEL
Well, it seems we cannot very well settle the color of the mountains intersubjectively.

MARCELINO
We were not going to use intersubjectivity to settle things in the first place.

DON RAFAEL
To the contrary. But we were going to try to

settle intersubjectivity, today, in the hope of Divine Grace.

MARCELINO

It will not be a day of rest.

DON RAFAEL

I am not so sure. Though the great systems of philosophy like to rest as they can on objectivity or on subjectivity, never on intersubjectivity, we may consider complacently enough that most of the practical world rests on intersubjectivity alone. That may be alarming in itself. Sunday itself has no objective validity, and we do not, from either of our single subjectivities, project an intuition of Sunday, but here it is Sunday, and we are celebrating it in the proper spirit, whatever the calendar may say in its exteresting way.

MARCELINO

But can we ignore the darker side, Don Rafael? If I understand you, this category of the inter-subjective is bound to include the worst manifestations of the mass mind, mob exaltations and hysterias as Hitler and others I need not mention have worked them up. They are enough to make the whole category suspect, and cast a shadow on the mentality, say the emotional solidarity, of good causes, the Negro marches, folksinging, any *esprit de corps*. Even the mass mind as represented in the theatre, at the best of dramas, can easily be called sub-intellectual. Any actor can tell us that the audience, whatever the individuals might be elsewhere, is, taken together as an audience, fundamentally idiotic and responds to coaxing and tickling as naively as a baby.

DON RAFAEL

All this is true. And it goes to show the vastness of the category, its terrible reality, and how futile it would be to set a constant value on it. It is no more reliable than objectivity and subjectivity, and we have to take our chances, hunting for our values through the wildernesses of all three categories as best we can. Dangerous as it may be, I think the category of inter-subjectivity is as good a hunting ground for value as the others, if not better.

MARCELINO

What seems to make the danger is the mass mind, with or without manipulation by an evil force. How many subjectivities do we have to allow, in order to set up an intersubjectivity?

DON RAFAEL

One.

MARCELINO

One? It is not possible.

DON RAFAEL

Not logically or numerically, but in fact, yes. There is a very solid and permanent thing called the Soliloquy, in which the subjectivity addresses itself. Another time we may discuss the formalities of that situation, but let us now just say it exists, and often splendidly, as in Ramón Gomez de la Serna's letters to himself, and in Manuel Machado's dialogue between his younger and his older self.

MARCELINO

This is going to be awful, if we cannot treat the subjectivity as a constant unit.

DON RAFAEL

Not so awful. We may treat all the personages of a soliloquy, no matter how many, as tenses of the same noun.

MARCELINO

As a grammarian, I protest. Nouns do not have tenses.

DON RAFAEL

Not in language, but they do in fact. Will you at least admit the existence of the Soliloquy, so we can get on with our counting.

MARCELINO

Very well. And two subjectivities would constitute a dialogue.

DON RAFAEL

At least. How about three at a time?

MARCELINO

That is Horace's limit, and the limit in Greek tragedy. A fourth speaker is very awkward, in the same scene at least. I have tried it. It is hard to get him to do anything more than chip in.

DON RAFAEL

How about the chorus?

MARCELINO

Well, there is the chorus, sometimes divided but homogeneous enough. Why are we talking about Greek tragedy?

DON RAFAEL

You brought it up, but it makes a good example to work with. We may take it as normal that at any one time, or in any one scene, however multiple each subjectivity may be within itself, there are only three individual ones. After that, everything is massive, or innocent bystanding. After three comes the chorus, or something like a chorus: the group, the battalion, the party, the nation, humanity.

MARCELINO

And the audience?

DON RAFAEL

Yes, literally the audience, and metaphorically the audience, we ourselves or the mind in a philosophizing situation. There can be an audience of one, as in reading a book, or of thousands as at a football game. Even so, the normal situations of intersubjectivity are not very many, and I think we can list them neatly: the soliloquy, the dialogue between two or among three, the chorus, and the audience.

MARCELINO

How about the author?

DON RAFAEL

Of course, whether we mean artists and writers or God Himself. If we should live to work out a system we should have to extend it to the whole universe and settle all the relations of the soul or of groupings of souls, but just now, on a day of rest, we may renounce all that unwieldiness and take an easy case.

MARCELINO

By all means, the simplest possible.

DON RAFAEL

No. If it is too simple it will be laborious again. But at least let us not consider Greek tragedy or the drama in general, or the epic, since they contain a plurality of subjectivities within them, let us not take on even the novel, for the same reason, but take a lyric poem, which we can suppose has only one subjectivity expressed in it. It leaves us with only three subjectivities to consider, the one in the poem, the real one of the poet, and that of a single reader.

MARCELINO

Plus their transubstantiations.

DON RAFAEL

Yes, but at least our lyric poem is a simplified field of intersubjectivity. We have only the livingness of, say, Shelley writing, and not the livingnesses of Shakespeare writing, Hamlet struggling, and Ophelia sinking, all at once.

MARCELINO

Shelley is not going to be so simple a case, if we take him. We will have to take on the intersubjectivity between him and the lark and between him and the west wind.

DON RAFAEL

Not immediately, I should think. The subjectivity in those poems is a composite, but it is a kind of soliloquy and we can still speak of it roughly as a single term in the situation, until we get around to analyzing it. We also take Shelley the man as a single term, which in fact he most extravagantly was not, and we take the single reader as a single term, which he can scarcely be, but we suspend all those variables knowingly, which is reasonable.

MARCELINO

Even scientific.

DON RAFAEL

Yes. For this experiment we may even suspend Shelley the man entirely, or the biographical man in any poet. We take the man as already transubstantiated into the poet and think no more about him.

MARCELINO

And the reader?

DON RAFAEL

Even more so. Whoever he may be, we consider him transubstantiated into the capable and sympathetic reader of whatever poem it is. In the act of reading

82

he is not himself. We shall have trouble enough with him just as a reader, without dragging his biography into it.

MARCELINO

But at least the poem itself is plainly where the intersubjectivity is, whatever the subjectivities of poet and reader may be.

DON RAFAEL

Rather the field where it takes place or goes on. And it goes on as a mutual possession of livingness.

MARCELINO

But the poet surely possesses the livingness in one way and the reader in quite another.

DON RAFAEL

Of course. Their functions are bound to vary, and often very widely. Even forgetting the twentieth century, even transubstantiated into a reasonably timeless reader, I cannot read the *Iliad* as if I were a contemporary of Homer, with the sensibilities of the time and a Greek dialect as my native language. And there is the obvious difference that Homer did the composing of the *Iliad* and I did not. But here we must be careful. In the present actuality of reading, or we might say in the intersubjective livingness of the poem, there is no feeling or thought of the three thousand years that separate us, as there indeed might be, if the *Iliad* were only a history of the Trojan war and not a possession of heroic livingness. Also we must beware of taking the poet for the producer of the poem and the reader for its consumer. In the mutuality of the intersubjective field the poet is part reader and the reader is part poet.

MARCELINO

That reminds me of a nice passage in Longinus, where he says that one sign of the sublime is a

83

feeling of elation and great pride in the reader, as if he had written the poem himself.

DON RAFAEL

That is an excellent critical touchstone: is the critic proud of the poem or not? He may like a poem or admire it, and those are positive values, but the true masterpiece would be something he is personally very proud of.

MARCELINO

Even though he inevitably cannot know and feel the poem exactly as the poet did?

DON RAFAEL

Yes. We have to allow for approximations. The confusion is not very great. The poet himself realizes in the written poem only approximately the poem he first intended, and as a reader of his own poem he will probably know it more in terms of his intention than as what it has actually turned out to be. But, supposing the poem to be an interesting one, as we understand "interesting," it will contain a force of livingness great enough to compose all these variables, of the poet and his readers, into a kind of society whose elements all live together or cohabit, even when there is disaffection, as there normally is.

MARCELINO

It sounds a little like the magnetic force that Plato speaks of, that draws the reciter of Homer to Homer, and through the reciter all his audiences to Homer.

DON RAFAEL

Or to the Muse. The source of the power remains mysterious, rather impersonal, divine, if you like. But I think Plato is right about the manifestation of the power, that it attracts and composes, maintains the inter-subjective, and is essentially not divisive. The poet as a man is usually quarrelsome, often odious, and hopelessly self-centered, but not the force he carries.

MARCELINO

At least in the work of art itself the force works toward coherence, the reconciliation of differences. It composes, as you say.

DON RAFAEL

This is really Sunday thinking, a little too restful to be true. Within the work the force can also be explosive, it can overwhelm and inundate, it can behave like lightning, devastate and disrupt. Even in your Classical art, though its more violent behavior is rather a speciality of the Baroque and the Romantic.

MARCELINO

As in the Last Judgment of Michelangelo, a gesticulating sort of decomposition which I must say leaves me cold. Or angry and repelled. But if I were a good Catholic in a millennial frame of mind, no doubt I would feel like a participant in the feelings expressed, in its livingness, even proud of it, and then it could be said that on the basis of power or sheer energy the beholder is at one with the work, however multiple and dispersed the painting is in itself.

DON RAFAEL

Yes. You are simply unwilling to transubstantiate yourself into the sort of beholder who can enter into the rather convulsive intersubjectivity of that painting. You will not make the effort of imagination. But this kind of thing happens constantly, the beholder or reader is simply not interested in an extremely interesting work of art. Either he does not understand the intent of Michelangelo or he refuses to participate in it. And being a good beholder or reader is a matter of active participation, not mere sensitivity or perceptivity, let alone education in the history of the arts. But this situation has been very well, though not fully, explicated years ago by a former colleague of mine, in an essay I keep there on the table, *The Intent of the Artist*. Look at page 21, the paragraph beginning, "The intent . . . "

MARCELINO

"The intent, to resume what has been said in the foregoing exposition, is a spiritual radiation, an energizing power bearing on the totality of the work of art . . . ."

DON RAFAEL

That is nearly what we have been saying at greater length. Do you see much difference?

MARCELINO

Yes. He is more resolute than we have been about putting the subjectivity of the artist inside the work of art, or taking as central and essential that alienated subjectivity which is manifested in and throughout the work. That simplifies the situation considerably, if the reader or the audience has only that single subjectivity to reckon with.

DON RAFAEL

Or to collaborate with, in the intersubjective possession of livingness. That would be the essential and proper situation, though the reader commonly and quite naturally wonders about the personal subjectivity of the artist and may try to see or feel it through the manifest subjectivity, as if the style were the man. And often enough the artist himself intrudes on his alienated subjectivity, to express himself or a personal grievance, some bee in his bonnet. But those are human weaknesses that get into the act and are not the essential.

MARCELINO

Are we to be severe or indulgent with them, do you think?

DON RAFAEL

As we please. But just now let us ignore them.
We assume the intent as a force functioning inside the
work, regardless of how it gets there. As the work faces
in the direction of the reader it has an aspect my colleague
called extent.

MARCELINO

Which would be its communicability?

DON RAFAEL

Yes, but not only its intelligibility, like the
language the poet has in common with his readers, or the
habit of certain scales which the composer has in common
with his hearers, or any such convention. That is only a
common objective ground, as it were. The extent of a work
would include also a common subjective ground, a
congeniality.

MARCELINO

Would that derive from values and beliefs
held in common, from a common culture?

DON RAFAEL

I would not confine it to that. No doubt
within a common culture, within a century or generation,
within a group, the common experience and understanding
is such that communication is almost automatic. So the
ordinary art of any time or group is likely to be all extent,
all communicability, with virtually no intent. It is done by
reasonably well trained and skillful people whose subjectivity, insofar as it is manifest in their work, at least, is
identical with the subjectivity of the time or the group.
The work is thus a sort of soliloquy, the group talking to
itself. It is still intersubjective, as we said the soliloquy is,
but it is only a relation between two duplicate subjectivities,
and not very exciting. One might even say that in very

commonplace art the subjectivity of the artist is not even a duplicate, but a kind of reflection in a mirror, with no behavior of its own.

MARCELINO
Is that very bad?

DON RAFAEL
No, but very limited, and easily abused. This is where propaganda takes place, for better or for worse, and the highly proficient brainwashing of the mass media, the best sellers, and so on. The skills employed are often admirable, even a great deal of intelligence is required, but it all goes into the extent. The intent, if any, is not a distinct or different subjectivity, but only a reflex of the subjectivity of the audience. If there is, as there often is, an intention to influence or mislead or dominate the subjectivity of the audience, that intention does not constitute a subjectivity but a simple objective practicality.

MARCELINO
But the popular arts can be delightful, very lively and exciting.

DON RAFAEL
Exactly, and they are becoming more so every day. But they are like the crystal in motion we were talking about, very lively indeed but without livingness. The fashion for what are called *happenings* is exactly the isolation and intensification of liveliness, without livingness.

MARCELINO
I think you underestimate the happenings. They do programmatically disrupt the overorganized practicality of modern life, and they might precisely disengage a livingness from ordinary experience, as sport and art can do.

88

DON RAFAEL

Perhaps they might, but I think they dis-
engage only liveliness, by concentration on the outer event,
on the communicability of the arbitrary fact, on simple
extent. And they are minority propaganda.

MARCELINO

But how can the serious artist, if he must have
a distinct subjectivity of his own, extricate it from the
subjectivity of his time and group?

DON RAFAEL

I hope you mean, not his own private subjectivity, but a different subjectivity functioning in his
work. Well, it is not entirely different from the subjectivity
of his audience, the spirit of his time and group, but it still
is different, at least another subjectivity, for all they
inevitably have in common. My colleague makes a useful
distinction between separation and separateness in the
artist. If the artist is really separated from his group and
time he is simply out of communication altogether, a really
alienated case, and his art is lacking in its essential extent.
Separateness is something else. It often takes the form of a
misfortune, though not an entirely incapacitating one. My
colleague gives the examples of the blindness of Homer, the
deafness of Beethoven, the madness of Lear. He might
have added the blindness of Milton, the madness of Blake
or Hölderlin, the invalidism of Pope, and so on. He
mentions the poverty of Cervantes. He might have
mentioned the exile of Dante and Shelley, the insane sense
of dispossession in Tasso, and the imprisonment of
Cervantes, Tasso, and others. All such separatenesses
prevent the subjectivity of the artist from being entirely
absorbed in that of his life and time, they force his subjectivity beyond it but not altogether away from it. And his

functioning subjectivity is forced to come at least partly from outside it.

MARCELINO

That is perfectly traditional, surely. The Muse comes from outside. She is not an Athenian citizen.

DON RAFAEL

But she is not quite a stranger either. We might call her a frequent visitor and even a metic, but by no means a citizen. Her communicability is immense, in excellent Greek, though with just the trace of an accent.

MARCELINO

An Olympian accent, one might say, not really foreign.

DON RAFAEL

At any rate, the functioning subjectivity of our kind of artist is neither properly his own nor that of his group and time, though all three are more or less of a kind. They are on speaking terms with each other.

MARCELINO

Sometimes not.

DON RAFAEL

And all three can quarrel among themselves. Both the Muse and his audience can abandon the poet, and he them. It is not always a peaceable relationship.

MARCELINO

But what is there, really, outside of his group and time, to accommodate the separateness of the artist?

DON RAFAEL

How can you ask? There is the whole range of the imagination, part of which he is commonly forced to explore. This is really unlimited, since it is the greater part of the universal Somethingness we were once talking about, and that included the impossible as well as the potential, the trivial as well as the portentous, and even the Uninteresting. These unending enormities and incidents beyond the actual group and time are a quite common recourse, especially when they are referred to as God or Nature. The religious dimension, no doubt the most common, is not confined to the theology or mythology of the group, nor is Nature confined to the scientific knowledge of the group and time. For the artist, the divine and the natural are far from confined to the rational. In that connection, my colleague quotes King Lear, who proposes to Cordelia that they "take upon's the mystery of things, as if we were God's spies." As a spy of God, the artist is indeed looking at, or rather into, the world of his time, inside it but from outside of it, and notice that he also takes upon him "the mystery of things." He may be forced to take it upon himself, but think of what the enormity of that mystery must have been to the mind of Shakespeare in such a time as his. The scale and complexity must have been nearly what we are forced to see in "the mystery of things" now. I would say that the functioning subjectivity of the artist, his intent, is a livingness as we have supposed, but also an acute aliveness, not to any specific thing, but to many dimensions of Somethingness at large, the imaginary and the indefinite as well as the practical and concrete. His livingness is considerably in excess of the life of the group and time and its occasions, of the communicability of the extent.

MARCELINO

We are, it seems, taking the Romantic view, of the artist as an angel strayed among us, or an albatross whose giant wings keep him from walking on deck like an ordinary sailor, as a sensibility too fine for the workaday world.

Don Rafael

The Romantics exaggerated a little, but they were not mistaken. The poet does live in excess of the practical order and in a way he invalidates it, so Plato quite reasonably proposed to get rid of him. But the poet is a good deal more than an eccentric and a public nuisance. His livingness goes on in areas of somethingness which the ordinary members of his group and time have had to abandon or renounce, though not entirely. Flaubert remarked that in every bourgeois there is the débris of a poet. We may add there is also an atrophied child, since the adult has had to restrict and deny the direct and indiscriminate livingness of the child or adolescent, which the artist maintains into adult life and age and all the more complex and practical experiences of life. Many great artists, like Shelley or Mozart or Tasso, are regularly called eternal children, but of course they are not children, it is only that they have retained much more of the unrestricted livingness of children than other people. But other people have had it, as children, and retain something of it. Even bank presidents do. And it is not at all that the artist takes his audience back into its lost childhood or lost innocence, but that he restores to them a wide and rash livingness which they deny themselves in adult life. It is not only the artist who lives in excess of the group and time; everyone does in some degree, but not with the fullness of the artist or poet.

Marcelino

Any bank president, any mainly practical man, would certainly think that any such full livingness is an escape from the serious business of the world, a vacation or a sport, whose main value would be in refreshing your mind for heightened efficiency in the practical world.

DON RAFAEL

The arts can of course be taken that way. But
for the artist himself the escape is really not from the
practical world but the contrary, an escape from the unlimited world of Somethingness into the circumscribed
world of his group and time. Often the brilliance of a work
of art consists in the shock or relief of arriving in the
comprehensible world from wandering about in outer
somethingness.

MARCELINO

You say the brilliance, but we might say also
the technical clumsiness or irregularity of the original
artist, compared to the perfection and smoothness, facile
or not, of his followers or others who live comfortably
enough inside their group and time.

DON RAFAEL

Yes, but we cannot well make a fixed criterion
of that, between the inside and the outside artist. Most of
the greatest artists are both at once. Shakespeare had
many predecessors in form, Mozart even more, and
Cervantes. Cervantes was an outside artist very un-
willingly, and in the end, in the *Persiles and Sigismunda*,
came back inside. But now we have come to other aspects
of the work of art, and rather objective aspects for a
change, the form, the content, the subject matter.

MARCELINO
Now we are getting somewhere.

DON RAFAEL
At least that is how the artist feels about it,
if we can trust Shakespeare's phrase about a local habitation and a name. But there is more in the habitation than
airy nothing, or the indefinite something which is the source
of the intent.

MARCELINO

Still, the intent ought to be dominant, a *genius loci.* or the spirit of the thing. Your colleague said, "an energizing power bearing on the totality of the work of art." Do you still agree?

DON RAFAEL

Very nearly. The power does more than *bear* on all the elements of the work of art. He was writing compendiously. As an *energizing* power it can saturate some elements, animate or magnetize others, distort and transform still others, but generally subsists as the livingness pervading the whole. He says somewhere that it "accentuates" livingness; I would say it *is* the livingness, and only appears to "accentuate livingness" when it animates or inflects an unliving subject or convention, like a given story or iambic pentameter, into an expression of itself.

MARCELINO

But even under the influence, or pervaded by the intent, the objective or conventional elements of the content and of the extent are the most distinct and obvious things to the attention, much clearer than the intent, and one might say they have a greater reality.

DON RAFAEL

One might say so, as one defers to objective reality. At least one usually likes to have a little of it around, even in the most subjective work. But its amount and its function and its degree of tractability to the intent all vary from one work to another. That is clear enough even in sport. In baseball you have the objective commonplace of the field, the diamond of bases, the bats and balls and, what is most illuminating, the uniforms. The players themselves are not themselves explicitly. None of them goes to bat wearing a necktie in his personal taste, unless he is a clown. The private subjectivity is put aside in the locker room. Another subjectivity replaces it, that special force that reveals itself, not in the objective uniform, which only serves to isolate it and heighten it, but in the style and prowess of performance. And that is what makes the most intense interest of the ball game, whatever the score. And the fans, though they are clear about the spatial progress of things on the diamond and may have bets on the merely numerical outcome, have, play by play, a very intimate sense of the special style and prowess of the players, and the situation is intersubjective—though God forbid we should say so to a baseball fan. If we told him he is as proud of a home run as if he had made it himself—

MARCELINO
If we spoke instead to a balletomane about a dancer—

DON RAFAEL
He would no doubt tell us more than we care to know. He would be as articulate as the baseball fan about the *extent* of the performance—the evident body, the conventional positions and steps, the excellence of their execution, the sheer athleticism of it in the given space and timing—but then he would begin to tell us about the expression, the content, the genius, or whatever. He will be voluble but on the whole incoherent, and will try our patience and draw our malice, as the performer and interpreter of Homer provoked the sharpest irony of Socrates. It is not his fault. One can be quite articulate and rational enough about the extent, about technique, but nobody has much more than exclamation to apply to the intent, not even when it is directly influencing the technique. Anyone can tell when a piece of music is being played correctly or incorrectly, and a musician can say exactly what the errors or false notes are, but between an uninspired correct

rendition and an inspired correct rendition, what articulate difference is there? One can say the spirit is present or absent, and we can say the livingness is missed or possessed, and everyone will know what we mean, but nobody is being very articulate about it.

MARCELINO

I do not resign myself to that easily. I once thought that musical notations, with all the little dots and curves and bits of Italian, were very close to being an articulation of expression. Well, it seems they are not close enough. Orchestra conductors have a terrible time of it. I have heard one bark at the orchestra: "Play music, not notes!" Oddly enough, the orchestra then does play music. The difference has hardly been explained to them, but they know what it is, and it suddenly appears in every note they play.

DON RAFAEL

"Once more, with feeling." But it is not just feeling in general. That wag Erik Satie gave very amusing indications in his piano scores, such as "white" or "interrogatively" but they are quite accurate. One can tell when his *Gnossienne* is being played pink instead of white, or only hesitantly instead of interrogatively. Even so, we must admit there is a distortion of the intent in communication, whether or not it has to go through an interpreter—like a piano player or a reciter. Even from the side of the artist, the articulation of his intent in the form is imperfect, considering the intractability of words and scales and meters however freely manipulated, and yet, within a certain tolerance, something very like the original "energizing force" does come all the way through to the audience.

MARCELINO

It is still rather vague.

96

DON RAFAEL

It is bound to be, like the soul. Still, there is a recognizable force such as the Homeric. There is the Keatsian. There is the Dantesque. The Hugolian. The Shakespearean. Even the Whitmanesque and the Dickinsonian. These words can be used to mean a style, or a certain range of ideas and materials, but they can also be used to mean a spirit, a mentality, an intent, whether or not we refer also to the content which it suffuses.

MARCELINO

And we do not refer to the private persons whose names we use in such words?

DON RAFAEL

In a general way, no. But we cannot altogether exclude them. They will get into the act now and then, and after all some quality of the private man is retained or transposed in the spirit of the poet proper at its most impersonal.

MARCELINO

Well, does the intrusion of the private subjectivity of the poet into the work of art disturb the more general intersubjectivity of it?

DON RAFAEL

That depends. It is a little like talking about one's self in conversation. It can kill the conversation if badly done, or it can enliven the conversation, if done with tact and humor, as if the private subjectivity of the speaker belonged to another person, which we may say it actually does. In such a case, what Rimbaud said is true, *je est un autre*. But the disguises and functions of the private subjectivity are very many. He can pretend to be objectivity itself. He can pretend to be any or all nine of the Muses. He can even pretend to be the audience.

MARCELINO
A joker in the pack.

DON RAFAEL
Yes, or a Harlequin. In my notebook there you should find a sketch under the heading "Dialogues of the Symbols, or Dialogues on the Circus." I did not get far with it, but I might have written it, so after all it is something. And there you will find the subjectivity listed among the clowns.

MARCELINO
Yes. You note he has many changes of costume.

DON RAFAEL
And the clown who represents Objective Truth has only one costume, white, with big black buttons.

MARCELINO
And Intersubjectivity is a blue clown.

DON RAFAEL
With spangles.

MARCELINO
Which reflect?

DON RAFAEL
And glitter in themselves.

MARCELINO
Do you mean him to be like a night sky?

DON RAFAEL
Very probably.

MARCELINO
Did you work out any acts for them?

DON RAFAEL

I only began to imagine them. And dialogues. Though the white clown, the objective one, is essentially a monologuist, uttering absolute and lonely truths. In the center ring.

MARCELINO

And the subjective clown, the Harlequin?

DON RAFAEL

All over the place, but always at an odd angle, in a corner. He speaks so to say from his own angle. His vision is in angle shots. *Verdades de rincón*. But he sees the absurdity of the white clown in the center ring.

MARCELINO

And the blue clown, with his spangles, would reflect them both in an irregular way and see the absurdity of both?

DON RAFAEL

Yes, the absurdity, but the absurdity can be either funny or sad. As clowns are both. And in turn the white clown and the Harlequin can ignore the blue clown and tell him he does not seriously exist. Especially the white clown, whom I see made up as a skull.

MARCELINO

But if he looks like a skull—a white skull with black holes for eyes—how does he get into an act of livingness?

DON RAFAEL

As Death does. As Objectivity does. My circus would have been one of great scope, really the big top.

MARCELINO

But would it have been a symbol of art, or of life?

DON RAFAEL

I suppose it could have been read both ways. Life, but life seen from the point of view of livingness, which I take for the point of view of art. My colleague called art a symbolical possession of life. Well, the possession is through a certain intercourse with its livingness, which becomes common to both, so my symbol might have meant the couple.

MARCELINO

Don Rafael, be careful. I see a school of criticism which could evaluate possessions of that kind, from frigidity, flirtatiousness, tenderness, Don Juanism, and so on, all the way to rape.

DON RAFAEL

It might be excellent criticism. But I leave it to you. I prefer to remember my circus.

MARCELINO

Were there animal acts?

DON RAFAEL

Naturally. And trapeze acts. By the great Baroque artists.

MARCELINO

And a freak show?

DON RAFAEL

On the side, yes. But the main show is the main show. It features lady bareback riders, by the way, and ladies who hang by their teeth pretending to be butterflies.

MARCELINO

And lady lion-tamers?

DON RAFAEL

Of course. And each clown sees them very differently.

MARCELINO

I should think the white clown would be reduced to silence.

DON RAFAEL

No. But anything he might find to say, from the point of view of Death or Objectivity, would have to be very funny.

MARCELINO

He would announce the mortality, the ultimate futility, of both ladies and lions. Or he would lecture on gynecology and zoology.

DON RAFAEL

With perfect truth and with perfect irrelevance. But see how he heightens or underscores the livingness of the lion-taming act! Objectivity is perhaps our most indispensable clown.

MARCELINO

Perhaps you will write those dialogues some day.

DON RAFAEL

Or you will.

MARCELINO

Badly. I am very unhandy with symbols.

DON RAFAEL

But they are simply objects put to an inter-subjective use.

MARCELINO

And very dangerous, like many uses of inter-subjectivity.

DON RAFAEL

I forgot. We need a dangerous clown.

MARCELINO

No, you did not forget. On your list is a
destructive clown, one who lights into things and tears
them to pieces.

DON RAFAEL

Yes, *diabluras*, devilment. He will have to have
a red costume, so nobody can mistake him. The circus
would be unreal if we left him out.

MARCELINO

You sound as if you meant to write those
dialogues.

DON RAFAEL

I have more serious things to do. And with
the Devil in them I should not even think of them on a
Sunday.

FOUR DIALOGUES ON
THEATRE

Dialogue One

MARCELINO
Good afternoon.

DON RAFAEL
A very good afternoon, Marcelino. But you sound unsteady.

MARCELINO
Unsteady? I have the outright shakes. Last night—

DON RAFAEL
You said you were going to the theatre, young man.

MARCELINO
That is where I went. And never again!

DON RAFAEL
I thought you were just beginning to write for it.

MARCELINO
That is another question. I am through with going to it.

DON RAFAEL
Sit down, make yourself a drink, and be sensible. One play cannot have set you against all theatre for good.

MARCELINO

This one did. It was a case of the coming theatre, Don Rafael, which, God help us all, has come! And I think to stay. The show has invaded the house, occupied it, actors, scenery, props, and all. Even the lighting no longer keeps to the stage, against a dark house, so you can concentrate on what is going on. It flashes about everywhere at random, goes out and changes color as if it were a drama in itself, a light show. There are projections, from behind, as if we also had several simultaneous movies, which do not move, or move spastically. Or a slide lecture with no lecture. Instead of thought there is sound, stereophonic, electronic, aleatory, and hideous. I think my hearing is permanently impaired. In short, Don Rafael, the show is so completely all over the place that the only safe spot left for the audience is, I assure you, out the nearest exit.

DON RAFAEL

You sound involved.

MARCELINO

Involved is what *they* call it. I call it trapped, battered, and generally roughed up.

DON RAFAEL

Was it well done?

MARCELINO

Yes! The technical proficiency was astounding. Even as a victim I have to admire the equipment of that torture chamber. It worked to perfection, except only that I got out alive and am not going back.

DON RAFAEL

It sounds interesting.

MARCELINO

Mangled as I am, how can I deny it was interesting?

DON RAFAEL

As theory, I mean. The Theatre of Cruelty may be interesting again, now it has seriously thought of taking the audience for its victim, and a physical victim.

MARCELINO

All right, Don Rafacl. As you no longer go to the theatre you may safely and theoretically take it for an amusing switch: instead of watching the characters suffer the audience does the suffering itself for a change. And fair enough. But when my actual net experience in the theatre is little but pain, anger, and hatred, I am not much delighted by the paradox. If Antonin Artaud is at the bottom of it, I say he was plain crazy.

DON RAFAEL

Not plain, Marcelino, fancy; wrong perhaps but as careful as Aristotle on the subject, maniacally precise. He too had something, as firm a footing on as wide a tract of Somethingness. If you refuse him outright you narrow your mind. Don't. And practically, if you do mean to write plays, why restrict your materials in advance? Why should not pain, anger, and hatred be included in your repertory of forces to be worked?

MARCELINO

I have not lost my head, Don Rafael, not entirely. I know they cannot well be excluded. In melodrama, and in propaganda theatre, or in the theatre of protest they are aroused in the audience. Of course, but they are directed against the System, or the villain, or any sort of evil. They should not be passions in the play directed against the audience.

DON RAFAEL
Why not?

MARCELINO
For one thing, a healthy audience would react by strangling the actors to death and burning the theatre down. As I felt like doing.

DON RAFAEL
That is only a practical consideration. Suppose the forces do turn back against the play: a self-destroying form is a form, and an interesting one, like suicide.

MARCELINO
Ontologically yes, yes it is something. But I no more enjoy watching a form destroy itself than I would a man killing himself, or getting himself killed by an outraged audience. There are limits to my *Schadenfreude*.

DON RAFAEL
You need not overdo it, but even your hedonistic prejudices must allow for the joy of destruction— including the ecstasy of self-destruction—as a major force, and consider its use in your theatre.

MARCELINO
God forbid!

DON RAFAEL
Theologically speaking, I very much doubt He will. I prefer not to call the force divine, but at least it is diabolic and must have its due. You remember that red clown in my symbolical circus? He is part of your business.

MARCELINO
If he pulls the whole tent down over my head?

DON RAFAEL
I am afraid so.

MARCELINO

You are not. You are being an *advocatus*
diaboli.

DON RAFAEL

No. Besides, a devil's advocate does not
advocate the devil, he only defends the claims of his client
to the soul of a prospective saint.

MARCELINO

Then why not his claims to the soul of the
theatre? Somebody should. They must be indefensible, but
until I hear an excellent lawyer—far sharper than poor
howling Artaud—defend them, and fail, how I am to feel
sure they are?

DON RAFAEL

If Artaud's howling deafens you to his
argument, that is too bad. Nobody else is likely to satisfy
you, not until the Devil himself defends his claims in
person.

MARCELINO

Short of that, why not you? You sound like a
cardinal when you please, or a devil's advocate, why not
like the Devil himself? I would listen.

DON RAFAEL

Extemporize in the person of my own red
clown? Yes, but over one horn I shall wear a red biretta,
too, and speak *ex cathedra*. Then you may laugh but you will
believe what I say, as ever. I shall whisper and hiss
insinuatingly, not howl, my poor innocent Marcelino, and
you will listen.

MARCELINO

Very well, I asked for this. But having raised
the Devil, I can circumscribe him.

DON RAFAEL
You can try.

MARCELINO
Here goes! Until recently the Spirit of Destruction had its place and served a useful purpose. It was understood to be revolutionary, to destroy a bad order and make way for a better, to break eggs in view of magnificent omelets. Now it is becoming an end in itself, with a mystique of its own, which ignores its proper limits.

DON RAFAEL
What are they? And why should the theatre fix them? Whatever God may mean by turning me loose in the universe, my claim to a dominant place in the theatre is validated by my dominant place in the universe—Nature, if you like, whose creatures destroy each other and which everlastingly destroys itself. And in your civilization—to confine myself to a narrower circle—who do you think inspires self-destruction in technology, and the increasing treatment of everyone, men, women, and children, as expendable? What is not disposable these days? Need I mention the Bomb? A form of theatre which destroys itself would be a symbol of all that, an elaboration of the primordial death dance, which was essentially what Artaud tried to recreate. A ritual celebration of *me*, if you like, and very legitimate.

MARCELINO
Good! What overwhelming authority from all sides! On it, such a form would even convey tragic terror and pity. And for a professor it would come under what we call in rhetoric "Romantic irony" and be classified beyond question. Legitimate! Bravo! But then I would say, as a conservative, as a bourgeois, as a rhetorician, that everything depends on how your symbol is handled, on how

much of its potential meaning it is actually made to express, cash down. If somebody paints a picture and burns it up, constructs something and blows it up, builds a machine which batters itself to pieces, or mounts a play that disintegrates into real life or a disorderly romp in the house, any intended reference to a larger meaning—to Universal Destruction, or Aboriginal Nada reclaiming all human effort and Art itself, or to Industrialism and the whole Paramilitary Establishment of Consumption and Waste—is certainly lost in the annoyance of the immediate and intensely particular event. The reference is extraneous, a footnote, or an obviously forged licence for otherwise insignificant vandalism. There may be a higher Vandalism, but this kind of thing is mere delinquency and bad behavior, at best a tantrum.

Don Rafael

Alas, yes. We poor devils have, often, to work with cheap materials, but our principles hold. When virtue is no more than good behavior, bad behavior is the appropriate means of demolition. Against complacency a tantrum will do.

Marcelino

Instead of a power of darkness you are being a power of obfuscation. You surely have to distinguish between an offensive prank and radical wickedness, between simple stinkers and serious Anarchists, between a hysteric and Attila?

Don Rafael
I do, but they all serve my purpose.

Marcelino
Not mine!

Don Rafael
If your purpose is still the threatre, it is subject to mine.

MARCELINO

The theatre is not yours, not essentially! Don't tell me it is originally, celebrating the dismemberment of Dionysus, the crucifixion of Christ, the massacre of the Innocents, the pranks and misbehavior of Satyrs or Devils, the burning of heretics—

DON RAFAEL

I would not dream of such a thing. I waive the many traditions which validate my claims. I stand on mere actuality: your performance last night.

MARCELINO
My performance?

DON RAFAEL
Yours, in collaboration with the show.

MARCELINO
I did not collaborate!

DON RAFAEL
You said you did. You wanted to strangle the actors. There you are: in the intersubjective transaction of the theatre you did your part. You communed, ritually, with Universal Destruction.

MARCELINO
But I did not strangle the actors!

DON RAFAEL
In your intention, you did. As the communicant intends to chew the body and drink the blood of Jesus. Overtly, of course, he is not a cannibal.

MARCELINO
There is something wrong with this argument.

DON RAFAEL
Of course. Whom do you take me for? Who

else confuses religion and theatre? But I only abuse a genuine likeness.

MARCELINO

Well, I take it as dogma that they are both intersubjective transactions, whether good or evil passions are exchanged. But once we had another such dogma, that the purpose of art, like that of religion, was the possession of livingness. The play or whatever it was I saw did not get me into possession of livingness, though it followed the Living Theatre of Julian Beck. They do talk and talk, with conviction, about Life in the theatre now, and they generally get as far as liveliness. Then something goes wrong.

DON RAFAEL

We had a trinity of terms and more or less distinguished them: Life, Liveliness, and Livingness. You say the show had liveliness?

MARCELINO

And to spare.

DON RAFAEL

But we observed once that liveliness can exist with or without a living soul behind it. We assumed that, Schelling or Novalis to the contrary, a crystal has no soul, however lively the agitation of that crystal may be in light. There was more to your show?

MARCELINO

Yes. We called that kind of liveliness exteresting, and the show was interesting, all too interesting. I was, damn it, involved.

DON RAFAEL

If it had belonged to the Theatre of Exteresting Liveliness, you would surely have had no objection.

What would the purest or most obvious form of such theatre be—for something to check against.

MARCELINO

Off hand, I should say the circus. The performers do have souls, even the trained animals do, I suppose, but the liveliness is essentially physical. One wants it that way: if the death-defying trapeze artist starts indulging his soul, expressing himself, making himself personally interesting, we are in for it, and so is he. One is intensely exterested in his performance, but prefers not to be interested, involved.

DON RAFAEL

Entertained in the highest degree, but subjectively disengaged. Could we simply call that kind of show entertainment?

MARCELINO

It sounds clear, the usual word, though we restrict it a little with our jargon—exteresting, liveliness, objective—

DON RAFAEL

But we cannot restrict entertainment to the circus. There are also carnivals, the diversions of a Luna Park or Coney Island, such as the fun house, the tunnel of horrors, the hall of distorting mirrors; then masked balls, spectacular dance numbers, and so on. Nor can we exclude it from the regular theatre. There are patter pieces, the farces of Feydeau or comedies made up all of epigrams and clever switches. And Shaw, in dead earnest, cannot help being far more entertaining than involving. But even in the midst of deeply moving drama, in the rhetoric of Aeschylus, of Calderón, often of Shakespeare and the Jacobean dramatists, the flights and turns and schemes of thought are an entertainment in themselves, a kind of trapeze work. So we distinguish entertainment, but we cannot exclude

114

it from any particular kind of theatre. Not yet. Nor have we begun to describe its variety of uses in combination with other things. Even so, can we say there was plenty of entertainment in the show you saw?

MARCELINO
There were all the makings of an entertainment, certainly, but I was not entertained.

DON RAFAEL
Perhaps because the essential of what we call entertainment—detachment, got lost in the shuffle?

MARCELINO
Deliberately. Life was supposed to replace it.

DON RAFAEL
But, according to you, not livingness. How did that happen?

MARCELINO
I wonder. Is livingness an abstraction from life?

DON RAFAEL
I would say so.

MARCELINO
Then so would I. The livingness intrinsic to any experience, even to that experience, never got abstracted, never came loose or clear. It never got off the ground. Here is a symptom: I was not allowed to forget myself, that is, my ordinary self, and perhaps as a consequence the people in the play were never characters or figures to me but only actors making a living or expressing and exhibiting themselves or, like children, making believe. For all the immense technique, it felt like a bad rehearsal.

DON RAFAEL
One thing at a time. Forget the actors a moment and tell me what you mean by your ordinary self.

115

MARCELINO

The self I wear to the bank. Not my casual or intimate or subjective self, whatever that is. I did put in an appearance, objective and overt. I wore evening clothes, though not a tuxedo. Say my ordinary formal self.

DON RAFAEL

Not much of a disguise, scarcely even a uniform. You should have dressed up like Savonarola or Cromwell for the hostilities, and brought something to throw.

MARCELINO

If I had known it was going to be a carnival of some sort instead of a play, if I had dressed up as someone more emphatically not myself, perhaps everything would have come out happily.

DON RAFAEL

More than likely.

MARCELINO

As it was, I dressed as what I superficially am, an aging member of the Establishment with an academic past. That should make for anonymity: I forgo any individuality of dress and present myself as a generality—a gentleman in the audience like a few hundred others— which allows my very largely uncommitted subjectivity free play, to assume any form proposed and to go along with anything the stage wants to do. It can circulate—as Flaubert has it—at will. I could not circulate last night. Why not?

DON RAFAEL

The reason must be in part physical. If an actor comes in from behind you, or the person sitting next to you suddenly turns out to be a planted actor—indeed if you or anyone at all near you is addressed directly by an actor on the stage or in the house you become more or less acutely conscious of the fixed location of your body. Some say one's identity is first of all a bodily sense, of muscular reflex, effort, and so on. There is something in it—at least it helps to explain how it is that if your physical location is insisted on and exploited for effect in a show you are thrown back from your free and indefinite subjectivity to your limited and individual self. Location individuates and particularizes; there is no doubt of that in any theory. The director of the show last night must have known it or felt it and meant to drag your bourgeois self bodily into the theatrical experience or happening or whatever it was.

MARCELINO

He succeeded.

DON RAFAEL

By more ways than one: if your ears hurt, as you said, and your eyes were strained or ached from the flashing of lights, along with your muscles being braced against the sudden impingement of actors, you must have been as conscious of your bodily self as of events around you.

MARCELINO

I was conscious, more than of being positively involved, of not being able to get disengaged. Disentangled is more the word.

DON RAFAEL

Yes, as a bourgeois you wanted most to recover your decent distance as a mere witness or innocent bystander of the doings.

MARCELINO

No you don't. Even as a bourgeois I want to participate, but not physically. In the first place I am not essentially a bourgeois at the theatre, in spite of my evening clothes. It was the show which arbitrarily cast me in that part, or in the part of a political simpleton, or of a beast or a maniac at large. It is worse than merely being thrown back on one's own identity, it is the imposition of a series

117

of false identities, of masks which do not fit or are gross caricatures. It is like a hall of distorting mirrors.

DON RAFAEL

There is a kind of theatre which is a mirror of its public; why not a hall of distorting mirrors?

MARCELINO

It could be amusing, but the first condition of being entertained by distorting mirrors is being fairly sure of what you really look like, of your own identity, and in the theatre you are not.

DON RAFAEL

What if the show were announced as For The Middle Class Only, For Simpletons Only, For Maniacs Only . . . .

MARCELINO

In that case it might be entertaining. I would go prepared and not be disappointed. I would go in a sort of mental disguise.

DON RAFAEL

And if you expected to participate physically, if it were announced as a brawl or an orgy?

MARCELINO

If that were understood, and I were in the mood for it, I might have a very good time. But it would not be great theatre.

DON RAFAEL

On what ground, Sir, do you venture to exclude orgies, carnivals, and political demonstrations from great theatre, as you call it?

MARCELINO

It is hard to do. I will not exclude Aristophanes. But if great theatre includes those things or some-thing like them, it somehow transfigures them and cer-tainly does not confine itself to them.

DON RAFAEL

Sir, permit me a slight suspicion that what you mean by transfiguration is remoteness. What you mean by great theatre is historical theatre, or theatre so derivative it might as well be historical, something in a museum and under glass. To be kind I shall say cultural theatre. What if people today find cultural theatre only exteresting and need something more directly alive? What if the essential of their current experience, its livingness, can be most vividly possessed—theatrized, if you don't mind the word—in forms like the brawl, the orgy, or the political demon-stration?

MARCELINO

For all I know they succeed in possessing livingness. Certainly a wonderful time was had last night, by the cast. Not, however, by me.

DON RAFAEL

I daresay you were not alone, and the audience was hopelessly divided. The intersubjective transaction did not fully succeed, in spite of your homicidal response. Well, there is a theatrical contract like the social one, but even less explicit, so these misunderstandings are very common. The intent of the play and the intent of the audience are often wide of each other, especially in a society where there is little solidarity or common under-standing about anything.

MARCELINO

But if the established conventions of the theatre are kept up, there is what you call an extent, a formal communicability, where the two intents ought to be able to meet, if not agree.

DON RAFAEL

No doubt, but a convention soon becomes conventional in a bad sense, an obstruction to livingness or a transaction of livingness instead of a conductor. The proscenium, for instance, which was a kind of tennis net for the transaction, begins to feel like a wall.

MARCELINO

So you scrap the proscenium and play tennis without a net?

DON RAFAEL

No doubt you try, for a while, until you can think of another game, like hockey.

MARCELINO

Religion, and now hockey! Can't we discuss theatre in its own terms? I may go with the wrong understanding, but I do not expect the theatre to be a game, least of all a bodily one. I want it to be a matter of souls, not of bodies.

DON RAFAEL
So do I.

MARCELINO
You are out of character.

DON RAFAEL

Not at all. The business of the Devil is much more with the soul than with the body. *Vilia corpora*, I always say, though so well aware of what uses they can be put to for the conquest of souls. A theatre of entertaining bodies is all very well, but too easy, and so is the theatre of interested bodies. Where I can really circulate with pleasure and profit is a theatre of embodied souls on the stage and disembodied souls in the house.

MARCELINO

Yes, I prefer to be disembodied. In the theatre.

DON RAFAEL

As I prefer you to be, reduced or raised to a
state of no special identity, to a generality, as you put it.
It is a very subtle process, which I find congenial.

MARCELINO

Is it a secret?

DON RAFAEL

No, but so familiar it passes unnoticed and
might as well be. It starts casually. You or anyone else
looks up a show to go to, in a paper, say, and the character
of the title attracts or repels or makes you curious, even
without reviews, and according to your dominant mood just
then in real life you choose which play. From either real
exuberance or real depression and fatigue you may select a
comedy. Or you may be having an excess of practical
energy, feel a need to come to grips with it all, and take on
a tragedy. Feeling a need to improve yourself, you may go
in a mood of docility to an unfamiliar classic. Feeling a
need to be abreast of things, you may select a current hit
which has rave notices. And so on. Though you go in the
first place for some sort of change, you bring with you a
general mood to be met. It is an abstraction, a kind of key-
signature or background coloration. It is a product of real
life, deeply conditioned by what kind of day the Thursday
or Saturday has been for you, but instead of changing it or
shaking it off as you would in real life you prolong it, all
the way from real life to the theatre, and it begins to
subsist in itself, disengaged not only from real life but from
your habitual self, and belongs rather to your anticipation
of the play. If you have selected something called *The
Downfall of Everything*, you arrive at the theatre in pro-
visional accord with it. You will hardly skip up to the box

121

office or wink at the cashier, unless you are exceptionally nervous. You will have changed your clothes, removed a lemon yellow polka dot tie and put on a dark one, to maintain the mood and make of yourself its appropriate vehicle. Your bodily bearing and dress imply a tentative agreement between your preliminary intent and whatever that intent of *The Downfall of Everything* turns out to be, within the promise of that title. This is only the beginning of an intersubjective transaction, but it is a beginning. If you have not really signed the contract on buying your ticket, you have at least acquired an option. But you are still not entirely transfigured or disembodied from a private and independent person into a "party"—into a participating member of the audience and nothing more. You are still in the lobby.

MARCELINO
Smoking and pacing.

DON RAFAEL
If so, the cigarette is a farewell kiss to your own body. But more interesting by far, you look around at other prospective members of the audience, for the last time in their individual forms, before their disembodiment. If you meet friends among them, the chatter is as exhilarated as that before the departure of a ship or plane.

MARCELINO
Yes, at once very gay and very sad. Very affectionate, even between casual acquaintances.

DON RAFAEL
And intersubjective.

MARCELINO
So it is, and that may make it a form of theatre in itself. Talk in the lobby is often better than the

play, just as a bon-voyage party can be the best part of a trip. I shall find it hard to renounce going to lobbies.

DON RAFAEL

Why renounce it? Go to lobbies and skip the plays. What of dressing rooms and greenrooms? As the lobby is a place of transformation for the audience before it goes "in," the dressing room is a place of transformation for actors before they go "on." A greenroom is a sort of mixture of the two, the actors being at once people and characters and the visitors being at once people and members of the audience. In a way the new theatre has very adroitly moved the greenroom into the house. Do you mind?

MARCELINO

I mind the confusion. I go to see a play. I like side shows as well as circuses, but not a side show with no circus or trying to pass for a circus.

DON RAFAEL

You want the lobby before the play, and the dressing rooms and greenroom kept separate.

MARCELINO

As they traditionally are. I see no reason to change them.

DON RAFAEL

I do. But for your kind of theatre I do need the lobby as a distinct place for the audience to transform itself and become disembodied, as I need the porch or narthex of a church. The church locates the stages of the process a little differently, but at least the holy water font is at the entrance of the nave and does something for the prospective communicant, as intimately as surrendering his ticket at the door. Temporarily he has renounced the world. When it comes to communion itself, remember that the communicant has confessed his sins and been absolved. He is, roughly speaking, in a state of innocence. Or of generality, having shed the particularities of his life, and assumed no disguise either, under which his usual self might lurk, in full possession of itself. He is a soul pure and simple, sincere if you like and generically a human, hardly even a man, woman, or child specifically. And very comparably, what actors think is the imbecility of the audience is the generalized state of its humanity. To maintain that generalization the member of the audience should be kept unaware of his body, very comfortably seated and all but invisible in the dark, since if he is looked at or feels in danger of being looked at he becomes conscious of his body. But detached from it, and from the context of real life which clings to it, the soul is now born again, fresh as a daisy, ready and available for whatever impression I care to make on it.

MARCELINO
Poor dear thing!

DON RAFAEL
It does not feel that way. It feels there is safety in numbers. Indeed we should not be talking about a single soul, since the audience notoriously shares what is called a mass mind, perhaps a collective innocence like the community of saints. How many people does it take to make a proper audience in your theatre?

MARCELINO
More than one. I feel very sure of that, and whenever I doubt it I remember a story told by Bernard Faÿ. His friend Count Etienne de Beaumont had a rather precarious theatre, a ballet theatre, in Paris years ago, and one evening Faÿ went with him to the theatre just before curtain time. They found the house entirely empty except for the dowager countess of Beaumont and a few of her

cronies in a loge at the back. She called out happily to her son—"Etienne, I wanted to surprise you. To help you out, I bought up all the tickets for tonight. I just haven't had the time to send them around to people, it was too wearisome. But no matter, you have a full house!"

DON RAFAEL

An exemplary story, with a dozen morals! For one thing, the lady cannot possibly divest herself of being the Dowager Countess of Beaumont and, in our sense of the term, reach a state of innocence, especially when the show is a personal and expensive hobby of dear Etienne's.

MARCELINO

How could one decently presume that the Dowager Countess of Beaumont would care to be a generality, a collectivity, or even disembodied?

DON RAFAEL

For another thing, she is virtually alone in the house, and that isolation can only keep her aware of her identity, her place in a very substantial emptiness. Her few old friends, who have known her identity for many years, can only keep her the more unalterably the Dowager Countess. If they were strangers and not sitting close to her it would be a little better, but not much. It takes at least a few dozen people, mostly strangers to each other, to create an anonymity and a mass mind.

MARCELINO

Well, does it? Sometimes I dream of a theatre like the private one at Nohant, in the house of George Sand. It could not have seated more than a dozen people, all guests and known to each other. The show was normally of puppets, manipulated by her son Maurice. He had made the puppets and she the costumes, hundreds of them. But their guest list is the great thing, the audience which might have been there all together at the same time, though most likely not: Flaubert, Turgenev, the singer Pauline Viardot, Chopin, the younger Dumas and a Prince Bonaparte! Can you imagine a better audience?

DON RAFAEL

Except for the countess of Beaumont I cannot imagine one worse! At least for serious theatre. Even for private theatricals, for intimate theatre, how did poor Maurice endure it?

MARCELINO

He was the great great grandson of the Marshal, Maurice de Saxe.

DON RAFAEL

That explains it, but otherwise an all-star audience is harder on a play than an all-star cast. And that particular guest list is made up not only of highly individualized personalities from real life, painfully public figures, but of highly developed imaginations, all specialized according to several particular arts, even politics, in the case of the Bonaparte. How can you reduce all that to a mass mind, even to a common sensibility at a high level, convivial as they would have been? Not that one wants the audience, as a collectivity, to be homogeneous throughout, and one welcomes a few such singular people in it, with their specialties and exceptional gifts, but one needs a good proportion of average people as a solvent, and a fair number of quite stupid people.

MARCELINO
Not too many!

DON RAFAEL

No, but they do assure the common humanity of the audience at large, its human nature, if you will, which has to be capable of stupidity, though not stupidity itself. Somebody in the audience ought to follow the motivations of a fool on the stage, even of an idiot, with fairly complete sympathy. And who else will feel that the foolish mistakes of Lear, of Oedipus, of Othello, are perfectly normal behavior? Not an audience of infallible intellectuals, I assure you. But if there is a positive ingredient of stupidity in the conglomerate mind of the audience, the intellectuals stand a much greater chance of possessing the livingness of folly, in comedy or tragedy, and conversely, the intellectual ingredient allows the average or stupid members of the audience to follow the motivations of rarefied characters on the stage more closely, with more sympathy, at least with a kind of unnatural patience. With a properly mixed audience, Hamlet himself is not lost on the pit, and the most vulgar of the fools and clowns can play directly to the stalls. To much the same purpose there should be a few scoundrels in the audience, a few nuns or the equivalent, rich and poor, and certainly some of the military. Though it is in a trance of innocence before curtain-time and is, in actuality, quite blank, it has ready a potential response to the impending stage events much greater than the potential of any single member. They all have as it were a pooled resource of emotion, a common fund of imagination on which they draw. Each draws unequally perhaps, and may have a private account on the side, but the common fund is, or can be, huge. You must like that metaphor, Marcelino, better than religion and sports.

MARCELINO
Frankly, I do. It makes it very clear to me why I vaguely felt robbed of something when the play last night reduced me to my individual self. To my private account. I was excluded, oddly enough, not involved. Emotionally bounced, sent out of the house to recover my identity where I checked it with my coat and hat, in the

lobby. Or as if I had been sent back from the very rail of communion to the confessional, to recover my individual collection of sins. Excommunicated, no less!

DON RAFAEL
Very well. Financially, socially, or religiously put, the audience is collective and a generality. You agree?

MARCELINO
Yes, perfectly. And now that we have the audience settled, innocent but with huge resources ready to invest, shall we raise the curtain and get on with the play? Or the transaction?

DON RAFAEL
I have not the heart to go on. I have been leading you astray.

MARCELINO
Perhaps, but I like it here. What is wrong?

DON RAFAEL
Have you no suspicion this is not great theatre, whatever happens on the stage? In Greek theatre, Elizabethan theatre, in the Spanish theatre of the Golden Age, there was no such house and no such audience. The plays were more or less in the open, in broad daylight, the audience came as it was, each member saw the others clearly and was seen. They were noisy, they ate and drank and threw things, they often engaged in little seductions of their own, whatever the play might offer. They were not in a trance of innocence.

MARCELINO
How did I forget all that? Why did I listen to you? Where are we?

DON RAFAEL

In the bourgeois theatre, of illusion, un-
reality, and escape.

MARCELINO

No no no. And if so, it is still the theatre I
shall write for. There is much more to be said for it. Damn
the Greeks and all traditional theatre.

DON RAFAEL

This is not your day to be temperate, Marcelino. Make us another drink and let us talk about
politics, a simpler kind of theatre and easy on the mind, like
melodrama. About the other kinds, yes, there is much
more to be said, and too much for today.

Dialogue Two

MARCELINO

Was nothing you said yesterday true?

DON RAFAEL

I was being the Father of Lies, of course, but those were very specious lies, I think, very close to the truth. Or what I think is the truth.

MARCELINO

It must be close to the truth that an audience is a collectivity. Everybody says so. But is it a random collection of individuals, as it seems to have been in Greece, England, and Spain, or is it a generalized humanity, as you so convincingly said it was in the regular bourgeois theatre?

DON RAFAEL

I confess that I think the audience was a generalized humanity in Greece, England, and Spain as well, but that in those periods the audience did not have to go through such a process of transformation to become a generality. The audiences were pretty well generalized on arrival.

MARCELINO

I know that, to judge from paintings and sculpture, almost all fifth-century Greeks look just alike, and so do Elizabethan Englishmen, and seventeenth-century Spaniards. But they must have had faces of their own.

DON RAFAEL

I doubt it, but if they did I think they did not feel it, except for a few extraordinary noses, like that of Socrates or that of Queen Elizabeth. I think they felt they looked very much alike, but the important thing is that they all felt alike. They had almost exactly the same passions and opinions, no very eccentric ideas or special sensibilities. You must have learned in school and often taught that the very special individual is a Romantic invention and developed through the nineteenth century.

MARCELINO

But Elizabethan England was full of remarkable individuals with distinctive careers. And there were important and very deep religious differences—

DON RAFAEL

As there were not in Greece and Spain. No, a general accord on religious matters, or on intellectual matters (as when in seventeenth-century France everyone, including Jesuits, Jansenists, and even Huguenots, was above all dogmatically rational) is not the only basis for a general identity in the people of such periods. Have you never been embarrassed by the fact, and made the least you could of it at the lectern, that all of the great epochs of theatre have occurred in imperialist nations, during the formation or consolidation of their empires—Athens, England, Spain, and, in her way, France?

MARCELINO
Yes, regrettably.

DON RAFAEL

It is hard not to infer that the formation of an empire is the first condition of great drama. Whatever the morality of it, the whole nation is engaged in action, usually action reaching far beyond its own borders, and every individual feels approximately the same about the public events—the battles, the voyages, the politics, the disasters. You do have remarkable and even unique individuals, but they are almost always adventurers, heroes or scoundrels, men primarily of action, and it is their actions or careers which are individual and unique rather than their private persons. You get a Themistocles and an Alcibiades, a Raleigh or a Drake, a Don Juan of Austria or a Charles the Fifth, and what they did is indeed unlike anything else, but subjectively they are only the mind of their nation intensified or exaggerated. Anyone in the nation could feel a participant in their extraordinary actions. And that subjective identity or participation in action—not in faith or thought, but in action—is specifically the ground of great theatre, if great theatre is drama, or action.

MARCELINO
I think it is.

DON RAFAEL
You would like to think so, but is this any time for it? America may be an empire struggling to consolidate itself, but does anybody feel that way about it except the great companies? Could you get an audience to feel that potassium or nitrates are a great incentive, as gold was to the Spanish? Anyhow, there are other kinds of theatre, happily, for the times in a nation's history when heroic action is not the center of its feeling. When an empire settles down into mere politics and administration, the theatre can still have a little action, but in the form of intrigue. Then it is not the action itself which is absorbing for the audience, but the complications and surprises of the intrigue, as in politics and administration. When even politics and administration become routine and of no interest, the theatre can still maintain a variety of action, simple activity, without drama or intrigue in the practical

sense, the dance. Not that I really think so, but let me say
that the dance is the beginning and the end, the alpha and
omega of theatre. It comes before the drama of imperial
action and after it. The theatre of the death dance, under
Artaud, who was providentially impressed with Balinese
dancing and derived everything he wanted from that
physical and mystical ritual, is perhaps the most essential
and comprehensive form of theatre.

MARCELINO
To hell with it!

DON RAFAEL
Of course! Thank you. But unhappily nobody
now takes the dance and the body seriously enough. I saw
Nijinsky often, and La Argentina, so I know very well
that in case of genius, a great soul pervading every inch
and moment, a single body can involve a large modern
audience in its expression of livingness, at as high a degree
of intensity as anything else in the theatre, but in general
the dance is only entertaining. There is a special public
for the ballet, which no doubt finds it more than entertaining or technically fascinating, even more than thrilling like
the stunts of a circus, but that public is a small and special
one, with very narrow responses. Nevertheless the fact
remains that if action and intrigue and the like are no
longer the prime realities of the subjectivity in real life,
inconsequential activity is real, and the dance embodies it.
To supplement the dance proper with a dance of lights, a
dance of words, a dance of musical sounds or random
noises, as your play did the other night, is a perfectly
reasonable attempt to enlarge the potential response in a
theatre of the dance, which in its way is very true to life
now, and might well appeal to the kind of audience we are
talking about, a generalized humanity.

133

MARCELINO
But it does not.

DON RAFAEL
It may in time. Why not now?

MARCELINO
Because the general public, including myself, does not like to think that action and intrigue are no longer real and that all we have left, subjectively, is inconsequential activity—or arbitrary happenings, objectively. We do not accept it and indeed we do not believe it. We still want action.

DON RAFAEL
Which is sentimental of you. And the residual bourgeois theatre is that. If you really believed in action you would not need all that hypnosis of a dark house, being brain-washed out of your identity and your sense of practical things as they are. In the Golden Age of Spain the conviction of action was so complete in the audience it was hard enough to get the audience seated, but next to impossible to keep it seated. Lope de Vega says he has to provide the seated Spaniard with all the action from Genesis to the Last Judgment—nothing less will hold his attention, what with the Holy Roman Empire and the Americas and the Indies and the Kingdom of God to be attended to outside the theatre.

MARCELINO
I suppose the Greek appetite for sets of tetralogies can be explained the same way, and the Elizabethan taste for several plots going on at once—

DON RAFAEL
Probably, and if we still had graduate students we could set them to worrying about how and why the action of the play is composed differently in each culture to suit the peculiar sense of action in the audience.

MARCELINO

And how the sense of action changes in the same audience, rather rapidly, when you think there is very little intrigue in Aeschylus and a very great deal in Sophocles. The *Oedipus*—

DON RAFAEL

—may be left to the graduate students you do not have. Just now we may take it that in those great theatres the audience was perfectly ready for action, but in the modern bourgeois theatre the audience has to be prepared. Still we may call it a constant that when the play starts the audience is ready for action. But is it active? Does it merely tag along with the stage action or respond to it, or does it do something of its own? It can heckle or applaud, throw eggs or roses, participate in that sense, but we are concerned with an intersubjective relation, with active or merely passive participation by the soul of the audience, which is in any case more or less a common one. What, if anything, does the common soul contribute to the transaction, either as perception or active imagination? How much can be expected of the common soul in any particular epoch? And what kind of thing?

MARCELINO

Well, in the Elizabethan Age it seems to have contributed almost all the scenery.

DON RAFAEL

And in Spain, where the costumes were splendid but the stage a blank. How would the imaginary scenery differ, do you think, in Spain and England?

MARCELINO

I leave that to *your* graduate students. Still, if the words are intended to guide or stimulate the imagination of the audience in providing the scenery, we could say that in England the scenery tends to be English and in Spain Spanish.

DON RAFAEL

How did we ever discover that?

MARCELINO

Erudition and ingenuity, Don Rafael. But I don't think it is so obvious. The scene is not always England or Spain. I mean that wherever the scene is in Shakespeare the words describe or suggest it in English terms, a lot of natural detail, in light, air, and especially weather. It is left reasonably wild in its natural context. But Spanish scenery is normally rhetorized beyond recognition, schematic, broad, simple, and empty.

DON RAFAEL

Do you think the seated Spaniard would have had the patience to supply all the lovely and aimless detail of English scenery?

MARCELINO

Certainly not. Is impatience the reason?

DON RAFAEL

One reason, at least, and the reason that in our Golden Age theatre the audience does not supply or care to follow anything like the lovely and aimless detail of English psychology.

MARCELINO

Well, how did the Elizabethan audience, surely as active as the Spanish, have the patience for it?

DON RAFAEL

I am not sure, but I think it is because the English were essentially colonizers, and not conquerors as we were. It is true that they did some conquering and we did some colonizing, but they were above all colonizers and traders, who were conquerors and pirates only as an avocation. Such was their patience and professional care for minute detail that they could colonize an empty stage with genuine English scenery and deal for five acts with so doubtful and intricate a customer as Hamlet. There cannot be such a character in a Spanish play. But however different their senses of what constitutes action, both audiences were very actively doing the part assigned to their imaginations by the plays.

MARCELINO

So were the Greeks. At least they were asked to imagine a vast amount of geography beyond the scene, or battlefields, or off-stage atrocities. But I have never felt sure how much psychology a Greek audience was supposed to follow or supply in the characters.

DON RAFAEL

How are we ever to know that? But we can be almost perfectly sure that in a Spanish character of the Golden Age there was no psychology at all.

MARCELINO

None in Don Juan?

DON RAFAEL

No. More recently people have spent a great deal of time trying to work out the psychology of the Don Juan type, but the character in the play contains nothing but a few very simple Spanish passions. Love, honor, revenge, and blasphemy almost make up our repertory. They do not have to be *followed* by the audience, or supplied, they are directly and unequivocally presented. And they do not develop; they simply assert themselves, constantly or again and again, as in a Spanish dance. Our drama is far too overt for the English. Obvious, if you like.

137

MARCELINO

A kind of façade of a drama, Baroque flourishes and all?

DON RAFAEL

No doubt. It is exterior, not an interiority like the English. When a character in an English play appears he "enters"—in a Spanish play he "comes out"—*sale*—as in a circus.

MARCELINO

Is Spanish drama only an entertainment then, as we agreed the circus was? How can it be intersubjective, if the subjectivity is all on the side of the audience and the stage is nothing but a very lively exteriority?

DON RAFAEL

I should have compared it to a bullfight rather than a circus. The torero "comes out" and certainly the bull does. The point is that the total subjectivity of the character in a Spanish play is present at each moment, which is in its way a moment of truth. Not the subjectivity in all the detail of its potential range, of course. I should have said the subjectivity as a totality, so any present passion in it has to be simple, complete, and when mixed at all a very rudimentary mixture. It is rather like a passion in an opera, full and vivid, but of no psychological interest. The audience responds to the expression directly, as to that of an aria, not much to the character expressing the passion, who is only its occasion or vehicle. The passion belongs rather to the common soul, the soul of the nation at that time, present as a potentiality both in the audience and on the stage, and its articulated passions are felt by the audience as its own, as if presented in a kind of emotional mirror. Someone said unkindly that Lope de Vega was the Bing Crosby of Spanish drama, and that is true enough; he expressed for the people at large their simplest feelings in their own style.

MARCELINO
Is it a limitation?

DON RAFAEL
Very much so. It has its peculiar and great intensities, but little depth or complexity in the Shakespearean manner. It is, however, a clearer case than most of the intersubjective situation in terms of livingness, as simple as the completion of an electric circuit. The plots and characters, like those of an opera, are simply conductors of the passions, not elaborated for their own interest or their likeness to real life. The livingness of the passions is disengaged from life or given a continuity of its own.

MARCELINO
But what is the function of the audience in maintaining it?

DON RAFAEL
Being totally present, ready with a complete response to the full expressions of the stage, to its own subjective image, if you like.

MARCELINO
It sounds like a Narcissist theatre.

DON RAFAEL
If you want to be psychological about it, yes. Don Juan is not a Narcissist, nor are the women of the play, but yes, the relation of the men and women in the audience to the characters is perfectly Narcissist. And so with the single figures in our dancing and bullfighting. Why be shy about it? Traditionally it is Stoicism, where the single individual is everything, or equal to everything, but for

modern psychology it is Narcissism—a very powerful force, by the way, which it would be foolish to deny or exclude from the theatre.

MARCELINO

It is proper to actors, at least.

DON RAFAEL

And to audiences. The audience goes to the theatre to realize or possess its own emotions. Or its own reality, as Artaud puts it. Why not, even if it possesses much more than that into the bargain?

MARCELINO

It sounds disreputable, yes, but why be nice about it?

DON RAFAEL

And to put it disreputably, the Shakespearean theatre is not Narcissist but voyeur. You get your kicks from watching the intimacies of other people. Hence the interiority I mentioned. Lear proposes that he and Cordelia look on at the world as if they were God's spies, which gives the relation a theological dignity, but it is voyeurism at bottom. Artaud said so; it must be true. More moderately I could say it comes from the English genius for detection. Perhaps on account of the fog it is a climate of secrecy and suspicion.

MARCELINO

And imagination.

DON RAFAEL

Naturally. But whether it peeks or peers or fancies it sees, the English audience looks on at something not its own. England is always a mixed case, so indeed Shakespeare wrote the chronicle plays and even *Lear* is in ancient England, but the scene is often in Italy or France or

Denmark or God knows where. It is, if you like, a theatre of diplomacy, implying the usual espionnage. In a word, voyeur. In a nicer word, a balcony—considered as an observation post. If Spanish theatre is a mirror, the English is a balcony. Which will you have?

MARCELINO
For plays of my own? For America? Neither seems quite right.

DON RAFAEL
How about the orgy?

MARCELINO
I have already refused it.

DON RAFAEL
You may come back to it.

MARCELINO
Perhaps, but just now I want to know distinctly what the audience is or does in relation to a regular play. An orgy is only a confusion.

DON RAFAEL
Confusion is something, and even a form, even a very contemporary form, with mixed media even in the theatre. But if you prefer clarity and simplicity, let us go back to the Narcissist audience, whether or not Spanish. In some degree and on some occasions it is in all theatre.

MARCELINO
We were saying that the audience has a common soul, which wants to look at either a reflection of itself or something else. Suppose there is a passion on the stage—enter an angry man—and suppose the audience responds to the anger, though it really has nothing to be angry about, is the feeling of anger in the audience the same as the anger of the character on stage, or the expression of

anger by the actor? Certainly not, but how alike are they and what is the difference?

DON RAFAEL

I am glad you do not call them identical, even if the passion is reflected or mirrored. To say the audience identifies with anything is very misleading. To say it sympathizes is not misleading but loose and limited. If we say the audience sympathizes with the character's anger, we seem to mean they understand the reason for it, and in his place would be angry too, and that is not necessary. The audience can sympathize with the anger by the mere sound of it or a gesture expressing it, without knowing the reason for it or thinking it a flaw in the character, to be forgiven or not under the circumstances. In that case it is anger in the abstract, as if it were an angry phrase in an instrumental piece of music.

MARCELINO

Yes, but anybody wants to know what the anger is all about. If it occurs in instrumental music one likes to have a program telling what Beethoven is so upset about, for example, even if it is nonsense.

DON RAFAEL

That depends on the audience, on how fiery or phlegmatic its temperament is, but yes, even an audience with very quick responses does like to have some idea of what the passion is about, even in the concert hall. In opera the occasion of the passion can be very perfunctory and even preposterous, almost any occasion will do, so long as there is some sign that the passion is motivated, and the audience, thus reassured, can feel with the anger in an imprecation aria, with the anger itself, forgetting its occasion.

MARCELINO

But the audience does not feel angry.

DON RAFAEL

No, and that is a standing theoretical puzzle. The audience, feeling with the anger, feels delighted, not angry, or at least the anger it feels is not the same as any anger it would feel in real life, all mixed up with complex occasions. Nor is it the same as the anger in the music, sung or played, though very close to it, in sympathy.

MARCELINO

It can work differently, when the audience is really angry. There is the story that Freud, when angered at the powers in Vienna, would sing to himself the fierce little aria of Figaro—"Se vuol' ballare." It expresses Figaro's anger at the Count, and no doubt Mozart's own anger at his impossible patrons, but it seems to have expressed, perfectly and intimately, Freud's anger too.

DON RAFAEL

No doubt all those angers resemble each other, as their occasions too are somewhat alike, yet they do vary, if only as intensities of the same force. Surely none of them is so intense as the combination of Freud's patriarchal fury and its heightening itself to itself by the more articulate scorn of Mozart's rhythm and da Ponte's stinging wit in the Italian words. Freud's anger certainly possessed itself, in a very paroxysm of livingness, by reflecting itself in the anger of the Mozart aria. It was the more intensely itself, and self-sustaining, by being reflexive, and one wonders if his actual grievances against the Viennese were not consumed and forgotten in the glare of it. But in that compounding of personal anger with artistic anger there is certainly, at that intensity, a new element, exhilaration. Or joy. As Aristotle says that tragedy is a pleasure, we could say that the possession of livingness, the livingness even of sinful passions and ugly ones, is exhilaration. It can be keyed up to ecstasy and so on, but let us soberly call it exhilaration.

MARCELINO

So Freud's experience would be an example of reflexive or mirrored passion—Narcissist. But it did not take place in a theatre. As I recall, he was waiting at a railroad station.

DON RAFAEL

It is still a good example. The original passion, or intent, is Freud's, he expresses it in a Mozart aria which closely corresponds to it, and he is his own audience. You said there cannot, but there can very well be an audience of one. But in the regular theatre, where the audience is not one but, we may say, at one, the play or the opera can try to reach the intensity of realization we assume in Freud's case—someone passionately singing or reciting to himself. When that happens, you have a hit.

MARCELINO

Not a masterpiece.

DON RAFAEL

Not necessarily. But you do have hits which last, which one may call masterpieces, and those which are good only for a season. Lope de Vega wrote innumerable hits, a few of which have lasted. Our question is how the hit manages to be so completely in accord with the feelings of the audience, deep or shallow, that the expression is reflexive.

MARCELINO

If only we knew that!

DON RAFAEL

We know a little about it and had better be careful of that little, however vulgar some of it is. We know we have to deal in commonplaces or topics, which we called universals when we were teaching, and these are especially the subjective universals—love, anger, fear, joy, sorrow, and the like. And these have to be carried, gener-

144

ally, by commonplace occasions—a woman, a wrong, a killer at large, a wedding, a death, and so on. All this, or some combination of generalities, does underlie the hit, but in the common soul of the audience the potential feeling of joy or anger has a limited range of intensities within the universal and a special responsiveness to occasions. An English audience, a Spanish, an American, an Italian, a German audience, will all differ in the quality of their joy or anger and in their sense of the adequate occasions. An audience of peasants or close to the peasantry will scarcely take to heart the misfortunes of a man who gives his land away—and to his daughters. Lear is beyond its sympathy, and his madness is strictly his own problem. But if the playwright keeps close to the temperament and prejudices of his audience, he is still a long way from a hit. Indeed if he keeps too close he loses novelty and surprise, which are essential, and in simple Narcissism, the mirror held too close produces only revulsion. So your problem is not easy.

MARCELINO

Well, I think it is not solved by the use of current issues, race problems, questions of particular wars and groups and institutions, on which an audience feels more or less alike and vividly. Such plays succeed in a way, but not in a big one. And why is that?

DON RAFAEL

You said once you did not like being cast as a bourgeois in the audience, that a false mask was forced on you. Nobody really likes it. The audience, like people in real life, prefers to feel itself a free agent, not to be taken for granted. That is why appeals to one's patriotism are so offensive, patriotic as one may be, or to one's better nature, though one be a saint. I think we were right in saying the audience is a generality, or a generalized humanity, though it would be a mistake to ask it directly to be human. Even a

145

Spanish audience does not care to think of itself as a Spanish audience. Even so general an identity is a constriction and an annoyance.

MARCELINO

Then how is one to appeal to an audience, if it has no identity in relation to the play and one cannot appeal directly to its prejudices or its emotions as if they were sure things?

DON RAFAEL

As Artaud asked, where do you take hold of it? He answered, by the body, but so far you want none of that. If you cannot get a good grip on it by the prejudices and standard emotions, which it resists, there is the problem of what you do to dispose of them, as your theatre disposes of the body, since after all they are there and cannot be kept out of the show.

MARCELINO

You said such generalities underlay the show or were latent in the responses of the innocent audience. Can they be treated as a groundwork or framework, even a proscenium?

DON RAFAEL

In your theatre, exactly as a proscenium, a common assumption by the audience and the play. The appeal is *through* the proscenium, not *to* it, and the attention of the audience is directed *through* it, not to it. General ideas should certainly be common assumptions, a proscenium, and not figure upstage or downstage. It is what goes on within them that makes the interest. New ideas, which are not yet common assumptions, are thus desperately difficult to stage in your theatre. But there is a great deal of didactic theatre, or class-room theatre, and there is the destruction of the proscenium, which ought to entail the abandonment of all common assumptions, ideal or emotional, and leave us with direct response to meaningless events, that is, with no frame of reference.

MARCELINO

Which it does.

DON RAFAEL

So in fact we have three kinds of theatre at least, two of them framed, like a mirror or balcony window, for the Narcissist and Voyeur functions, and a third which has no frame, and indeed is not so much visual as it is tactile and corporeal—an orgy, as we disreputably put it. Which will you have, if neither of the first two?

MARCELINO

There must be more. But why not the third, really? It repels me, but what is really wrong with it?

DON RAFAEL

The way we described it, a free-for-all of more or less direct sensations applied to the physical organism, it is a very limited form of theatre, a sort of play-pen for one's animal nature, and hardly more than real life. It is real life behaving very strangely, perhaps, but with little disengagement of livingness and no meaning for the mind. Yet there can be much more to it; it can be used as a basis for much more. Even the original Dionysiac orgy was a possession by a higher power of life and destruction alike, and reciprocally a possession of him, a very interesting communion. The orgy can have that kind of dimension, expressed in the bodily one, or the dance. The body moreover, which we said may be the source of the feeling of individual identity, is also amazingly uniform. For all the minor differences from one body to another, nothing is more monotonous than a nudist colony or a nudist beach, as I recall. But bodily actions and bodily responses to sensations are also very much alike, so that a theatre which is a downpour of sensations of all kinds can perfectly well reduce the audience to a generality, not a common soul, if you like, but a common body or a common bodily life, reacting simultaneously and all but identically, to the same physical stimulus of sound, sight, or touch. When Gloucester's eyes are plucked out, the audience winces as one body—

MARCELINO

But that, with all reverence to the Bard, is a cheap stage trick. It is played with grapes and sleight of hand by the actors and it is not real for the audience either, which conserves its eyesight.

DON RAFAEL

Does the body know that, singly or in common? At that moment, or those two moments, no. The mind may worry about the illusion later, at leisure, but during those moments the livingness of Gloucester's torture—not the real or factual torture—is possessed by the audience, and in its common body.

MARCELINO
And what of its mind?

DON RAFAEL
Well, what of it? Is it ever more alive and alert than at such moments? Artaud sometimes insisted on that, that it is the mind which is influenced and enlivened by the violences done in his theatre to the body or the bodily imagination. One can well take it as an ascetic theatre, legitimately given to mortification of the flesh, not for a perverse pleasure but for an intensified life of the spirit.

MARCELINO
So you say.

DON RAFAEL
And not inaccurately. I say spirit, soul if you

148

prefer, and not the articulate or discursive intellect under the guidance of words, as in your literary theatre. In Artaud's theatre the spirit moves through moments or a continuity of intuitions, both of bodily sensations and of the tempestuous forces which precipitate them in their irresistible onrush. Those forces are passional, natural, but also cosmic. They are Dionysiac. Words become only exclamations, wild cries, and are hurled with the force of solid objects, not abstract meanings.

MARCELINO
Which at least explains the use of obscenities in the theatre these days, of noises instead of music, of blinding lights instead of visibility. But seriously, how about this mysticism? When Artaud talks about cosmic forces, and magic, and alchemy, and all the rest of it, especially his infatuation with the Orient as a higher wisdom, my mind closes and stays closed.

DON RAFAEL
That is un-American of you. It is quite true that an Oriental theatre is essentially for an Oriental audience, and that a theatre whose proscenium of assumptions is composed of cosmic forces, magic, mysticism, alchemy, ritual and so on, is most interesting to Orientals or cultist amateurs of the Orient. To an American audience it can only be exotic and exteresting, a curiosity. But Greek, English, French, and Spanish theatre are also exotic to America, and do not require a very special audience, since the tradition of the country is not only mixed or international but hospitable.

MARCELINO
Within the Occident.

DON RAFAEL
Not strictly. The country is after all an

Oriental power as well as Occidental and soon enough the Chinese theatre will be no more exotic to you than Racine. You should prepare for it.

MARCELINO

It is a great effort. If the show the other night was Oriental in origin, interpreted through a crazy Frenchman, it seemed altogether American, a perfectly native piece of show business, to the point of being all technique, overemphasis, and superficial immediacy. I do not see how I could have framed it in Oriental assumptions even if I had recognized them.

DON RAFAEL

You had no sense of the cosmic forces raging through it? Well, perhaps they did not rage. No Yin? No Yang? There is your difficulty: the framing Mythology was not there to give the theatrical events and gestures a significance and an emotional resonance. Artaud saw the difficulty and said that the old myths, Occidental or Oriental, would no longer work, but the problem was to disengage the living forces they contained from the outworn formulas.

MARCELINO

And the solution?

DON RAFAEL

God knows. Artaud talks about poetry as the method. I suppose poetry would take on a cosmologizing function again, as it did with Hesiod and as your poet Charles Olson tries to make it do, as a projection, moreover, of the living body. We may hope.

MARCELINO

I do not. Artaud would not have meant a verbal poetry, or literature, which he wanted kept very subordinate in the theatre. He wanted a poetry of stage materials, but how can one construct or project a cosmology from those materials?

DON RAFAEL

That is for you to worry about, and whether your cosmos is going to be a play of forces or a structure or both, and how the audience is to know it. One pretty solution should have been the use of a real scene, a street or a square or a subway station, for a happening. Beyond the real scene extends the real cosmos, framing the event, and the audience is, I believe, dimly aware of it, since the scene is immediately and perceptibly open upon it or involved in it. But I am afraid the happening in the open was no more than entertaining, even when fairly violent. The Surrealists complain of it, that their most serious demonstrations in the real world were taken as only very amusing entertainments by the public.

MARCELINO

Even with some notion of the theory behind them and some sense of their poetic validity, I cannot take happenings seriously. The immediate effect is childish, an innocent parlor game conducted in the street, happily enough, or even on the open sea. They are nice, but I want a theatre that acts its age.

DON RAFAEL

If the mood is childish amusement, as at a circus or a fair, you have the generalized audience we posited for theatre, and an entertainment, which we have not excluded. And why should not the real cosmos be used as part of an entertainment? It is so used by the astronauts and so on, and the audience may have that sense of it in any part of it used as a scene.

MARCELINO

May we return to the real theatre?

DON RAFAEL
Or the unreal theatre?

MARCELINO ..
At least a theatre where imagination is the primary activity.

DON RAFAEL
But it takes a good deal of imagination to think up a happening.

MARCELINO
That is preliminary, part of the intent of the originators. The performance itself is perfectly concrete fact, and no great demand is made on the imagination of the audience or the secondary participants. The audience has no intent beyond that of going along with the gag.

DON RAFAEL
Very well. Let us leave happenings out of it, though wishing them well. We mean a theatre which is a collaboration, more or less continuous, more or less intimate, between two imaginations, that of the playwright and that of the audience, meeting on the material basis of the stage and staging.

MARCELINO
And words.

DON RAFAEL
Necessarily?

MARCELINO
No, but preferably.

DON RAFAEL
I must give you an assignment, my boy. Read Artaud.

Dialogue Three

MARCELINO
I am not convinced.

DON RAFAEL
You still believe in literary theatre?

MARCELINO
Yes.

DON RAFAEL
Exclusively?

MARCELINO
Of course not. Nor do I think the theatre should be simply the illustration of a literary text, a recitation with pantomime added. Artaud was right about that much, surely, and no doubt the French theatre in his time had become excessively verbal. There is not much to Giraudoux beyond the brilliance of a literary style. No doubt the silent movies or even the talkies had made so much of the drama of physical movement that the theatre had to insist on something of its own, verbalistics or literary drama. Be that as it may, I think the disjunction is a mistake, and even the subordination of the words to the staging is a mistake.

DON RAFAEL
May I say you believe in a mixed medium, then, but simply mixed, words and actors? Do you believe in scenery?

MARCELINO

Not much. But I believe in props which get into the act, and when scenery is as useful as that, I believe in it. Otherwise I like it left to the imagination, or made as perfunctory as the proscenium.

DON RAFAEL

That would depend on particular plays. But in general you want a theatre made substantially of words and actors?

MARCELINO

Yes. You make it sound restricted, but that is what I want.

DON RAFAEL

And what do you want the words to do?

MARCELINO

That is a long story.

DON RAFAEL

Yes, interminable. But we can skip a good deal of it. We need not say they can be used for exposition, for explaining the situations of a story, for presenting previous and future action, and so on. How do they make a ground for the intersubjective transaction we were going to describe—the collaboration of two imaginations, as we said?

MARCELINO

In a rudimentary and automatic way the mind of the audience supplies the meanings of the words to itself—supposing it knows the language. Can we count that function as imagination?

DON RAFAEL

No. I think we can call it understanding, but even so we may say the mind of the audience is participating in the play, more or less busily following the meaning as it goes along. It is not much but it is something, and indispensable. It belongs to the extent of the play. Then what?

MARCELINO

In our terms, the intent. Very close to immediate intelligibility is something actors know is the essential—motivation. It expresses, by inflection, loudness or softness, speed and timing and so on, what the character intends to accomplish by saying what he says and how he feels about it.

DON RAFAEL

Of course. It brings the subjectivity of the character into more or less direct relation to the mind of the audience, whether or not the subjectivity of the audience is engaged beyond mere understanding. The playwright may provide for motivation, and even indicate it in a note before the actual speech, but is this not really the actor's business, interpretation and expression, and not ours?

MARCELINO

As theorist and possible writer? Well, we have to take it into account, leaving a great deal to the imagination of the actor, whether we like it or not, but just the written words in themselves can convey a great deal of subjectivity.

DON RAFAEL

By their content?

MARCELINO

Yes, of course. By "woe is me" or discourse about feeling. But just in the verbal form, the rhetoric, whether the words are in prose or in verse, you get the expression of a subjectivity.

DON RAFAEL

Do we have to go into that?

MARCELINO

Perhaps not in theory, but in practice it is a perpetual question, even after you have decided in general to write in verse or prose.

DON RAFAEL

How do you decide that?

MARCELINO

It is not easy. It is often said that verse drama is dead, but it is not. Arthur Miller once wrote a play in verse and then reduced it to prose, in order not to make the actors uncomfortable or affected. There is a standing practical difficulty, the rarity of actors who can speak verse lines without sacrificing either the dramatic motivation or the formal quality of the verse.

DON RAFAEL

There is also a difficulty in authors, the rarity of the prodigies who can write verse that is not routine versification but has at once a poetic value and a dramatic one. T. S. Eliot knew all about that difficulty, whether or not he solved it.

MARCELINO

Nevertheless a great deal of verse drama is written, with all kinds of versification, and that must mean that the intent of many playwrights demands verse in its expression.

DON RAFAEL

I don't doubt it. But aside from the difficulty with actors, how about the difficulty with audiences? Is there a general audience which is subjectively affected by versification?

MARCELINO

Yes, if it is in the lyrics of a musical comedy or

revue. I am not sure of the present audiences of Shake-speare, whether they do or even should listen to the versification. In a musical comedy it is part of the entertainment and is listened to attentively, but if there is a serious song it is no doubt subordinate, a modest accompaniment which does not obtrude itself with remarkable effects. In the case of a play, a modern play, I am not sure of how much the versification reaches past the extent of the form into collaboration with the intent of any audience.

DON RAFAEL
With all those difficulties and uncertainties, do you mean to write plays in verse or in prose?

MARCELINO
In verse, damn it.

DON RAFAEL
You are perfectly right. If your intent demands verse and you get it articulated in the extent of a play, something is indeed lost on the audience, at least on a first performance, but a play should perhaps keep something in reserve for later performances, no matter how much is committed to collaboration on the first. In the case of a masterpiece there seems to be no end to the reserves, to the beauties of detail or even larger expression which one missed on even the tenth performance one attended, say, of *Lear* or of *Hamlet*. Still, the permeability of the extent should not depend at all heavily on verse, not now. Indeed, if the audience is aware that the play is in verse it will take a cultural attitude at best, prepare to admire a work of art as an object, as a solemn kind of entertainment, and be unavailable for the intersubjective situation. You still want to do it in verse?

MARCELINO
Yes. There are many devices. One could

begin by seducing the audience into participation in verse by a comic passage, even by a comic song, and then slyly change the tone, getting the audience gradually or abruptly into participation in tragic poetry. Or one could begin with prose, gradually increasing its rhetorical color and its regularity of beat until the audience can get into straight poetry, either without knowing it or as a pleasant surprise. The problem has to be handled with care, but it can be handled.

DON RAFAEL

But why poetry in the first place?

MARCELINO

I had rather call it verse, in the theatre, since the poetry of the theatre can pervade all its media, even the scenery. Well, I think I want verse mainly as a technique of abstraction. Prose is ordinarily an instrument of practical life, whereas verse is an instrument of living-ness—of poetry—when it succeeds.

DON RAFAEL

But verse can be deadly, and prose can quite well be an instrument of livingness.

MARCELINO

No doubt. There are the dangers of prosaic verse and poetical prose. In the hands of a great master, like Samuel Beckett, the prose is rhetorically so intensified, compressed, or distilled, that without being what one would care to call a prose poem it functions like poetry, conveying as violent a livingness. But for lesser writers and amateurs, verse is surely more promising. It keeps you headed toward the livingness of poetry, whether you get there or not. Prose is the hard way.

DON RAFAEL

But the safer convention in the theatre just

now. In either case, the verbal articulation should express livingness rather than life. Everybody says the language should be heightened or "sweetened" and we do not disagree, but we say in our terms that it should abstract the livingness from life. Do we not?

MARCELINO

We do. Not that we have settled all the special cases. I remember the most living moment I ever had in the theatre was the end of Racine's *Andromaque*, where the emotions are so extreme that the sleek and perfect alexandrines were the only safety in that storm, one clung to them for dear life, almost counting the syllables for reassurance. A more expressive versification would have been unendurable. But that play is an exception.

DON RAFAEL

But that use of very regular verse—as insulation—may be normal in your Greeks. Could you stand the *Agamemnon* or the *Oedipus* in great prose? And how about *Lear?* We may not want our livingness perfectly straight. In Spain we certainly wanted it tempered with liveliness. Instead of the everlasting English pentameter or French alexandrine, we wanted a great frequency of change in the verse forms and rhyme schemes, redondillas, hendecasyllabics, sonnets, even sestinas.

MARCELINO

Sestinas?

DON RAFAEL

Yes. You might think there could be no deader form, for sheer doggedly protracted ingenuity, but Lope uses it in one case to convey a sudden overwhelming joy, and his sestina maintains and augments that emotion for an incredible length. It is a virtuoso stunt, lively beyond belief, but it is used to sustain and increase a livingness. Still, I do not recommend the sestina to anyone who is not

Lope. All I mean is that if we are considering verse we must be careful not to restrict its uses in the expression of livingness to poetry proper—it can subserve, by its simple objective perfection or liveliness, a livingness which is not essentially verbal—the portentousness of a situation or an emotional extremity in a character. The verse may, but it need not, express such moments of livingness directly.

MARCELINO

It can leave the more direct expression to the voice or the gestures of an actor?

DON RAFAEL

Or to silence—as used by Aeschylus, Shakespeare, Beckett—

MARCELINO

Forcing the imagination of the audience into the act. Even so, I believe in words, in verse or prose, as the predominant and most continuous instrument of livingness. And as the habitual ground for the collaboration of the two imaginations.

DON RAFAEL

Are they a ground? Sometimes they are a glass, whether a mirror or a transparency. Remember that remark of Menander, which Racine made in his turn, that his new play was finished, and all he had left to do was write it. The substance of one kind of classical drama at least is people doing things, a composition of events and passions in conflict, and the words do nothing of their own, they merely make the substance apparent. Even the verse is colorless. The decorative epithet is a great rarity in Racine, if you can find so much as one, and the same with metaphors. For all the artificiality of the verse, its transparency is perfect.

MARCELINO
And Shakespeare?

DON RAFAEL
And Calderón? And the choruses of Greek tragedy? No, transparency is not their quality. I sometimes think Greek choruses were meant as a mental curtain, drawn over the raw livingness of the action at intervals, to let the audience recover itself. Very rich and sumptuous curtains they often are, and sometimes semi-transparent, like scrim, but they do not give the audience a direct vision of the passions in action, as the dialogue does. Or usually does. In short, the function of the words varies considerably. They can be hurled at the audience like solid objects, be an entertaining interlude in themselves, or a kind of gorgeous costume for the soul of a character, as they often are in Shakespeare, and the actor has to wear the words as much as speak them. Sometimes they provide imaginary scenery, but they can be a kind of scenery in themselves—fountains and fireworks. Sometimes, with bold figures, they are a drama in themselves. It amazes me how little I miss, not going to the theatre, but having the text of a play read to me. A play can as well be for the blind, or for the radio.

MARCELINO
You reassure me so much about literary theatre I am becoming uneasy. After all, it is the stage I shall write for, if I write.

DON RAFAEL
And for actors more than staging, I think you mean. Words and actors were to be the basic media. Do we know anything about acting?

MARCELINO
I do not. I have read about it and seen it and

161

even directed it a little, but the inside of it remains incomprehensible to me.

DON RAFAEL

We may leave it at that, and consider whatever method they are trained in not our business. Still, in our terms of intersubjectivity, we may know what we want of actors—namely the presentation of a living subjectivity to the eye and ear of the audience. Aside from elocution and seeming to understand the words they are saying, we want of them in particular a clear expression of the motivation of their words, the motion and movement of the soul of the character, and that expression is a temporal art very close to music, involving rhythm, phrasing, dynamics, tempo, even pitch and tone. You must provide for that by writing a kind of score into your wording. As to the actor's body, it should be that of a dancer, alive throughout. What Lope de Vega has an Englishman say of the Spanish in general we might say of the actors we hope for: ". . . a Spaniard, who holds everything in his soul. If they go on foot, the soul is in their feet; if they raise their hand, there is soul right there; if they move their proud body, it is soul."

MARCELINO

I think most actors are quite clear about that as it is.

DON RAFAEL

Very probably. But are playwrights? You have to write in a sort of choreography as well as a musical score. You can even be finicking about it, as Molière had every step made by his actors counted, and as to this day no actor of the Comédie Française may decently cross at the caesura of a verse. That is hardly worth observing in modern plays in English verse, but at least you should write with the mobile or moving actor in mind and not leave all the directing to the director. You need not pin him down with a lot of stage directions as they used to do, but the speaking text should by itself afford him a wealth of opportunities.

MARCELINO

Suppose that, one way or another, by choreography and gesture, by motivations expertly played, livingness abounds on the stage. What does the audience do about it?

DON RAFAEL

Ultimately you should ask a psychologist that. But practically I can say that as there is a sympathetic kinesthesia of the body there is a sympathetic kinesthesia of the soul. As one's muscles register or respond to the movements of a dancer one is watching, one's mind responds to the movements of the mind or soul of a character on the stage. And one keeps in time with both movements. The rigid present of stage time can make them as compulsive as a musical beat, as hard to resist as marching when, strolling along at your own pace, you suddenly hear a march being played. The play may and often does lose its audience; or it has to syncopate its rhythm slightly to keep an audience—which was responding slightly off the beat—still continuously responding. A scene may drag on one night and rush through too easily the next. That is the problem of directors and actors, but however it succeeds or fails, the play is a synchronization of the movements of feeling in the audience to those of the play. That much, I think, is rudimentary. Everything else is more complicated—how does one engage the feeling of the audience? By violence or enticement? Does one keep it engaged constantly, or release it and then recover it, and by what means? One must not forget that the audience likes to feel it is a free agent—not trapped, as you said you

163

felt—and moreover has a kind of emotional attention-span, and so cannot be held to the same feeling or the same pitch of feeling for very long. Goethe, both as a playwright and as a director and manager, recognized a law of obligatory change. He was certainly right, but the changes are not simply from solemn to light, from agitated to tranquil, and so on, but from intersubjective to objective, from involvement to entertainment and back. And there are degrees of involvement to be manipulated, and many qualities of entertainment. A continuous gripping climax for two hours or more may be an appealing absolute in theory, but not what the organism of the audience can stand.

MARCELINO

How sturdy an organism should I assume the audience is?

DON RAFAEL

A little sturdier than you imagine it is, but not of Olympic stamina. An audience likes to use its strength and to draw on its collective strength, but not to be overtaxed. If the demands on it make it feel the limits of its capacity too clearly it will begin to feel its individual identities, disengage itself, and be lost. The same way with demands on its intelligence—it enjoys intellectual effort, even a little mystery and bewilderment, but not a losing struggle with obscurity. Remember, too, in reckoning its emotional and intellectual capacities alike, that your generalized humanity still contains the residual differences between men and women, not counting children or the childish element in men and women. In traditional theatre there was a shrewd mixture of subjects—political issues for the men and a love story for the ladies, often with a political heroine like Clytemnestra, Lady Macbeth, or Cleopatra to keep them together. But the duration of the political material has to be roughly measured to the strength of emotion in the ladies tackling such material—as well as to their attention span and interest—and the duration of the episodes of the love story has to reckon with the patience of the men in the house. The feuding of the Capulets and Montagues makes the love story of Romeo and Juliet tolerable for a sturdy audience, as does the fact that Juliet is not Romeo's first love. She is also a remarkably precocious thirteen, since the audience is on the whole adult.

MARCELINO

What do you think of Schiller's idea of a theatre devoted entirely to tragedy and for men only one night a week?

DON RAFAEL

You know what I must think of it—appalling, even for one night. No, we assume a mixed audience for the increased range of emotion, and prepare for the given predominance of women. One can understand how Schiller felt about that, but one should not lose one's head and bounce the ladies altogether. They are stronger than we think or than they care to admit. Still, you should be more considerate than Aeschylus, who frightened them into miscarriages and little children to death.

MARCELINO

So the strength of the collective soul has its limits and is not constant. Its plenitude is soon spent and has to be replenished by rest or diversion, entertainment or what is called comic relief. And that soul is not unqualified humanity either; it is in a preliminary mood, and in response to actual stage events the genders and ages in it come more or less distinctly into play. Otherwise it is a quite indeterminate force, like the human mind or imagination in general. As a working assumption, will that do?

DON RAFAEL

I think it is safe enough.

MARCELINO

But how about what you called the embodied souls on the stage? They are usually very determinate, deep in their own peculiar psychology and the detail of their past and present conditions—

DON RAFAEL

Not in all theatre. Not in the Spanish, as I said. There are at least four kinds of theatre in that respect, not necessarily pure and mutually exclusive, but they can be distinguished. First, since we began that way, there is the theatre of souls, in which the characters are substantially souls and need have almost nothing in the way of psychology, morals, or intelligence. This may well come from the religious origins of theatre, but it is a permanent kind, subsisting in secular theatre, in Spain, and in Shakespeare, and even through the late Romantics— Rostand, Maeterlinck, Giraudoux. Then there is the theatre of types, where the characters are psychologies and moralities instead of souls. That begins, apparently, with your late Greeks like Menander, after the biological classifications of Aristotle and the Characters of Theophrastus. So we said in the classroom, but it seems to be true. Then there was the theory of humours in the Elizabethan Age, the revival of Classical types in seventeenth-century France, as with Molière's *L'Avare*, and in our time the use of Freudian types by O'Neill and Tennessee Williams and so on.

MARCELINO

Are they Freudian types or Freudian cases?

DON RAFAEL

That is a good distinction, but let us make it another time. Also, you might object that Hamlet is more than the embodiment of melancholia in general. You might

166

say he is equally a soul. Or equally a case. As I said, the kinds do not exclude each other.

MARCELINO

No. I was about to say that Harpagon in *L'Avare*, while a type of avarice well enough, has a soul, and a terrifying one, as does Tartuffe.

DON RAFAEL

Still, they are essentially, or distinctively, moral types. What they are may perhaps be decided by the kind of cosmos they inhabit, the full universe of nature and the supernatural or simply the social world. Souls have a distinct tendency to live in the universe while moral types live in the social world. At that rate Don Juan, who is perpetually treated as a moral or psychological type, and in either case a cautionary example, is in fact a soul. That is true also of Faust, in Marlowe as well as in Goethe.

MARCELINO

And how about psychological cases?

DON RAFAEL

Any handbook will tell you they live neither in the universe nor in society but in an environment. And they belong to another kind of theatre. But in the first two orders of theatre, that of souls and that of types, there is a difference in what the characters are up to. Souls work out a destiny in the universe, types succeed or fail within the social world.

MARCELINO

Yes, but there is a mediaeval sort of drama, which exhibits the destiny of souls in the cosmos of God, beyond society.

DON RAFAEL

They are not souls in our sense, but mere

types of sin and virtue, and they succeed or fail in the closed society of the mediaeval cosmos as simply as Tartuffe fails in the society of Louis XIV—more simply, in fact, since God was the more infallible monarch.

MARCELINO

Are the mediaeval types such a bad thing? I would agree they are, except that I was once astonished at how deeply moving a parade of the Seven Deadly Sins can be.

DON RAFAEL

Yes, one would expect them to be quite empty symbols by now, and very frigid theatre. I suppose what filled them with livingness was simply the powerful potential for each of the seven sins in the collective conscience of the audience. But symbolic or ritual theatre is still another kind, and not only mediaeval. It is with us in the political plays of Brecht and Sartre, where it is too easy to dismiss the characters as empty or two-dimensional types. They can be filled out by the collective soul of the audience, like the schematic characters in Spanish drama. The danger is that the audience of a mirror drama of the political kind may not recognize its own image or may refuse it—as you did.

MARCELINO

In any case I do not see myself writing political plays or morality plays of any kind. They are a kind, but the two kinds you mentioned, the theatre of souls in a cosmos and that of types in a society, sound more to the purpose just now. Except that souls, if given that name, may be a little unmarketable.

DON RAFAEL

More than a little. And that is not your only difficulty. I think we said a soul is a force and has no form of its own. If so, through what forms do you make it evident to the audience, or what articulate movements do you put it through so the soul of the audience can respond and perform its own kind of mimetics along with it?

MARCELINO

Sometimes it is given a dominant passion, which everybody understands.

DON RAFAEL

A passion, yes, rather than a vice or virtue, since we are dealing with forces. But if the ambition of Macbeth is a passion, say an expansiveness of the soul acquiring ever greater power—not only higher titles— there are two serious difficulties. What is to keep the nicer and more temperate souls in the audience from taking the soul of Macbeth as a bad example, a type of ambition understood to be a vice?

MARCELINO

Nothing, I suppose.

DON RAFAEL

And what is to keep the ambitious souls in the audience from taking Macbeth's soul as perfectly sympathetic, but composed only of the one passion, ambition?

MARCELINO

I suppose, nothing. Unless they have read that Shakespeare is a master of complex character-drawing and so Macbeth must have much more to his character than the one passion.

DON RAFAEL

Which makes him a psychological case instead of a soul. An objective study, as non-conductive as a cautionary example.

MARCELINO

In the classroom you can perhaps make Macbeth out a psychological study, but surely not in the theatre, at the quick of the events?

DON RAFAEL

You forget there are cultivated people at the theatre, and people who are there for cultural improvement. Part of the audience can quite well study Macbeth instead of miming the movements of his soul. And Shakespeare seems to provide for everybody.

MARCELINO

For us, souls with a passion.

DON RAFAEL

No doubt, but the passion is only a motive, a comprehensible motive, which sets the soul moving or acting. What you have in the rigid stage present, at the quick of events, as you call it, is the soul in movement, in action or simply in motion.

MARCELINO

Mere motion?

DON RAFAEL

Yes. In the big soliloquies, for example, you have, through the highly eventful poetry and the philosophical content, the motion of a soul. Any actor could tell us that. But whether the soul is in action, movement, or motion, whether only reflecting or engaged in conflict with circumstances and the movement of other souls, it is a substantial livingness, right there in the stage present— questions of its particular passion, its circumstances, its character, are only its conditions, and secondary. Even the ambition of Macbeth is secondary—incidentally induced by these witches, one might say—it certainly goes slack at times and is lost in the despair and desperate courage of his

170

end. He is a soul moving through a whole series of passions.

MARCELINO

Well, so is anybody.

DON RAFAEL

Precisely, which is why the collective soul of the audience, which is without any particular character and has no one governing passion, can move along with Macbeth, with excursions into Lady Macbeth, Duncan, MacDuff, and so on. In theatre of this kind our souls move together in a cosmos, as I said. You may not think Scotland is much of a cosmos, but it is enlarged indefinitely by the witches, the ghost of Banquo, the hallucination of Birnham wood and so on. It is large enough to accommodate the largest motions of the soul in its ultimate conditions—this world in general, with some encroachment by another. The sense of an unbounded world, or a world whose boundaries are indefinite, was perfectly natural, in times of empire, for Aeschylus, Shakespeare, and the Spanish, but we still have it. However local our characters and passions and intelligences may be, our souls inhabit the universe at large. How are you going to stage it?

MARCELINO

I will come to you for advice when the time comes. Or I shall study Thornton Wilder with more care. The action of *Our Town* is in the universe at large, not in a village. And *The Skin Of Our Teeth*—But if the soul needs all that space to move in, and really has nothing to do but go to meet its destiny, so that its passions and the development of its character, its successes and failures, are only episodes along the way, what makes it move in the first place? We have called it a force well enough, but what is its object—besides expending itself?

DON RAFAEL

Since this is a theatre of ultimates, I shall say

171

Being. Unamuno once made a little scheme of four kinds of souls, four different forces in relation to Being: one that wants to be, one that wants not to be, one that does not want to be, and one that does not want not to be. *Querer* is his word, more desire than want, if you like, but anyway a force. In this theatre, which we may as well call heroic theatre, the motion of the central soul in the play turns on how it desires or does not desire Being or Not-Being. The question of moral types, of humours, of particular passions, is all subsidiary to the behavior of the force in relation to Being.

MARCELINO
At least Hamlet, in his shuffle about to be or not to be, is not being a philosophy student just back from Germany, but a case of not wanting not to be.

DON RAFAEL
Plainly, but you have different stages of the force in motion. In Macbeth you have a long preliminary struggle to be, at all costs, a brief moment of being, and a long losing struggle to maintain it. In Othello, we begin with him as a great commander who desires to continue being just that, and then succumbs to a counterforce, one that desires not only not to be but that Being not be. Iago says nothing at the end. There is one of your silences that resound: Nothing. With Lear we have complete human being gradually and agonizingly disintegrated, one attribute at a time. As a king, he gives away his realm and all the honors too are taken from him. As a father, he is without children. As a man, he has the "mother"—or the hysteria belonging to women. As a rational animal, he loses his reason. As a natural creature, he can barely survive on the heath. There is the desire to be—"every inch a king"—struggling on all fronts against the Not-Being to which it is destined.

172

MARCELINO

Some say it is about filial ingratitude.

DON RAFAEL

You need not repeat it. But in ultimate
theatre, theatre on such a scale, there is evidently room
for schoolchildren. And plenty of it in the first act, which
begins like a fairy tale, two older sisters who are very
wicked, and one, the youngest, who is virtuous to a fault
and rather simple-minded. No, heroic theatre is inclusive,
at any rate with Shakespeare, and very odd things indeed
are included. But sustaining or carrying it all is the hero, a
force of some size, as Aristotle might say, directed toward
Being or Not-Being—usually toward being as much as
man can be or toward maintaining himself in being what he
is. In Spanish theatre this motive or intent is formulated
as *honor*, but less formally it is the motive of Don Juan,
who persists in being what he is to the death, and of Faust,
who wants to be everything mankind can be—in Goethe's
version at least—as well as to possess Being, symbolized as
Helen of Troy. For all the various embodiments of the
heroic theme and the variations on it, the theme varies very
little in itself, and is almost always a tragedy, for the simple
reason that the fullest Being that man can aspire to, within
the world at its largest—Nature and the natural powers,
if you like—ends in death.

MARCELINO

Is that a moral?

DON RAFAEL

No, it is rather a perspective of assumptions, a
proscenium of ideas. The substance of the play is the living
out of his life and death by whoever the hero is, within
those terms.

MARCELINO

Can we make that assumption now?

173

DON RAFAEL

I doubt it. Is any audience now likely to be
passionately interested in acquiring or maintaining Being
in the universe at large? Will it believe in heroes directly,
without adapting itself to the cultural conventions of past
theatre—a Greek or Elizabethan or whatever? A
believable modern hero on the traditional scale? And if
you presented one, would he not freeze the audience? Are
they likely to participate in his heroism naturally, without
sentimentality or embarrassment?

MARCELINO

So we give up heroic theatre for this epoch?

DON RAFAEL

No. The technical problems are immense, for
the theatre, but in life the materials are there as ever.
Man still has his desire to be or not to be, or his unwillingness to be or not to be, according to Unamuno's scheme.
And there is heroism all over the place. But in the theatre
the collective soul is shy of it, unwilling to believe what it
has to believe in real life or even the newspapers. But that
is your problem.

MARCELINO

The second order of theatre, of types in
society, not of souls in Nature, sounds easier.

DON RAFAEL

We said it was, but is it? The proscenium of
assumptions is in good repair. The adventures of the main
character—if we cannot call him a hero—go on within
society, and his motive is not toward Being in the universe,
but toward getting what he needs for success in society.
By society I mean not just polite society, but the whole
economic world, the business world and the world of the
very poor, where bare survival can be a social success and

174

a fortune. Does the audience have to be introduced to the conditions and motives of such a world, or can they be assumed?

MARCELINO

They are constantly assumed, and they ought to make for excellent mirror-theatre, insofar as the audience is a social creature.

DON RAFAEL

Then why does it make people restless?

MARCELINO

Perhaps because it has a message or seems to have one, as a commentary or a description of conditions.

DON RAFAEL

When it does have a message, even when it is an important message or the audience agrees with it heartily, the effect is somehow disappointing or irritating. But social theatre need not be didactic. There are innumerable parlor comedies and lyrical treatments of the impoverished, but they still, as social theatre, are not altogether satisfactory. They can be highly entertaining, in our sense, and sometimes sentimentally affecting, but if the characters are simply social types or social products, living only within the social proscenium, the audience is somehow disappointed, and why is that?

MARCELINO

I think they miss the livingness of individuality in the characters. Or so they say.

DON RAFAEL

But at least a liveliness of what you call individuality is often supplied by a good actor or actress, even in the most mechanical of parlor comedies. And a great actor can even provide livingness. But in that case

175

the play is simply a vehicle for the performer, which is all very well but not what we are after. In any case, whether in the actor or in the character proper, what do you mean by individuality? And is it individuality anyway, added into the social types, which would make a social theatre the sort of intersubjective transaction we were talking about?

MARCELINO
I am not sure.

DON RAFAEL
Nor am I. We had better meditate on the purest case of social theatre we know.

MARCELINO
Molière?

DON RAFAEL
Agreed.

Dialogue Four

DON RAFAEL
Well?

MARCELINO
I think I have discovered something. Molière's theatre is thoroughly social, and the characters are social types. Even when they are antisocial and eccentric, they are defined by society's view of them. The scene is everlastingly a human habitation—a salon mostly, and at the wildest a village, never a heath. Nevertheless, his theatre is really not contained in human society. His characters tend to be solitary and self-sustaining existences, for one thing, selfish and intensely self-willed. It is too early for the monads of Leibniz but they may be in the air, and at least self-love, *l'amour propre*, is the mainspring of the current psychology.

DON RAFAEL
I wonder why Molière never wrote a play called *The Altruist?* Such a character would have been even more eccentric in his world than *The Misanthrope*. But does the all but absolute egoism of the characters, their spring of self-love under their social type, give them an individuality?

MARCELINO
That is my discovery. It seems to. In spite of the fact that they have no personal biographies to speak of

and no mentalities of their own, no idiosyncrasies beyond the stock types of soubrette, scoundrel, young lover, miser, *raisonneur,* and so on, they do have wills of their own, so that on the stage, in the midst of the action, they present an almost violent individuality, to which one responds as to a vibration. One does not feel them as types, even in the slapstick farces where they are caricatures based on the *commedia dell' arte.*

DON RAFAEL
But, except for some variation in strength and in purpose, all the wills are identical?

MARCELINO
Yes, individual in the extreme, but identical.

DON RAFAEL
Like souls?

MARCELINO
I suppose so, in that respect, but smaller. Or more concentrated.

DON RAFAEL
Yes, at least they do keep to the point, and do not elaborate and ramble about in every direction like the people in Shakespeare. They are souls confined to the function of reasoning. Their reasoning is often hilariously mistaken, but it is what they obsessively do. Under the stock type there is self-will and reason—subjective forces which are also in the audience?

MARCELINO
Yes. Or so far so good. And we could call it fundamentally a mirror theatre, and intersubjective. Even Tartuffe is not altogether non-conductive, though his reasoning is in the form of scheming and his self-will toward larceny and ruthless power.

DON RAFAEL

An evil soul and a large one, complicated moreover by lust, but is he heroic? He may be a borderline case.

MARCELINO

He is really too large for being contained within society, and only the King can, in fact, contain him, and only in a secular way.

DON RAFAEL

What if we had a soliloquy in the manner of Shakespeare—Tartuffe at prayer, for example, or showing the real inner motion of his soul—?

MARCELINO

It would be Shakespeare, or Romantic theatre—cosmic or heroic theatre, not social. But there is a really ambiguous case, in *Le Misanthrope*. When Alceste makes his big final exit, to go live in the wilderness and renounce human society, his friends say they are going after him to change his mind. No doubt the last few lines are mainly to get the two friends off the stage, but they make Alceste's departure into the wilderness inconclusive to say the least, and probably mean he will come back. The lines are never heard in performance. I was once furious at the Comédie Française because I thought they had irresponsibly been cut, and when I met the actor, who was playing Alceste again with a company touring this country, I complained that as a professor I was shocked that those crucial lines were cut, both by the very conservative Comédie Française and by the touring company, giving the play a Romantic or open end. He said the lines were never cut, the actor spoke them very loudly, but they were never heard, because the audience always applauded the big exit speech of Alceste immediately and could not or would not hear of the possibility of his return. The last lines of the play have probably not been heard in the theatre since the Romantic movement, or perhaps the middle of the eighteenth century.

DON RAFAEL

So the intent of Molière does not correspond to the intent of later audiences, which supplies its own sense of outer Nature and makes the play subjectively larger than it was at first. But this kind of interference by the changing subjectivity of later audiences, and by our own, is perfectly normal. We allow for it. Still we may say that in theory there is a perfectly social theatre, and Molière is a very good and familiar example of it. And we would not, I think, be far off his intent in saying that the subjectivity of his characters, and that of his first audiences as well, is self-will and reasoning, directed to purely social issues and goods. Why should it seem to us so mechanical, so restricted?

MARCELINO

No doubt because Shakespeare's imagination is wilder and less subordinate to good sense, but even without that example haunting us we have acquired a great respect for the irrational, both in the human soul and in the universe at large. Also, alas, in politics.

DON RAFAEL

So that Reason, or the reasoning faculty in the characters and the audience, has not at all the same value with us as it had with Molière, in whose time Reason had not only conquered the universe and subjected it to its discipline of clear and distinct ideas, but reduced society and the human soul itself to a rather simple system of forms and motives. The whole immense enterprise of Reason, whether by Descartes alone in his room or by the collective mind of the century, was heroic, in our terms or any terms, a will to be, and on the cosmic scale. As any geometric truth was true on any scale, at a desk or in astronomical space, any assertion of reason about the smallest matter had its heroic bearing, some resonance of exploit, which is lost on us. All of this does not prevent us from entertaining a theory of strictly rational theatre, objective theatre. We were once agreed, I think, that objectivity is an attitude or function of the subjectivity, and can be the ground of our intersubjective transaction, not between two imaginations this time, but between two rationalities.

MARCELINO
But does an audience participate in objectivity or simply endure it, as a not very entertaining entertainment?

DON RAFAEL
It participates very readily, above all in comedy, and as a collective rationality. An irrationality, an absurdity of logic or fact presented on the stage, is what commonly draws the rationality of the audience into collaboration, and a living or lively one, for composing the comic event or gag which brings down the house. "We have changed all that" requires—and instantly gets—an act of objectivity on the part of the audience. We might call objectivity a force, at least in the theatre.

MARCELINO
I believe you did, when you invented that white clown with big black buttons. Why not defend his claims?

DON RAFAEL
I think I should, since they are in danger or ignored, when they could easily be extended to the whole theatre of the absurd, which depends on Reason to recognize the absurdities. But I confine myself to our

second order of theatre, the social, which deals not in souls but in rationalities, unreasonable as they may be, like that of Alceste. The audience, in this case, is a common nationality, even more innocent and impersonal than the common soul of heroic theatre, and instead of following the movements of passion by sympathy and imagination, it follows the development of a proposition, be it practical or philosophical or both, by its sense of reasonableness or logic. Sometimes the audience has to be guided through a rational tangle by a *raisonneur* or some such figure, as the feelings of the audience of heroic theatre seem to be guided through a tangle of passions by the Greek chorus or a confidant. But the action and the characters have to be rationally comprehensible. We get no demonic souls like Iago, whose practical motivation is unaccounted for, no moody undecided souls like Hamlet, no witches or visions, and certainly no such absurdity as a wholesale catastrophe turning on a lost handkerchief. It all has to stand to reason.

MARCELINO

But if it is all so practical and rational, what of livingness? I thought we had decided that livingness was in excess of the practical, if not of the rational.

DON RAFAEL

We said it was in any experience, to be abstracted, and insofar as reason is an experience—insofar as it is reasoning and not the mere result of reasoning—there is livingness in it, to be abstracted.

MARCELINO

Oh! Of course, there is the set debate in Greek comedy, the agon, ideas used as a sort of sporting event. And then the Platonic dialogue itself, which derives from the mime.

182

DON RAFAEL

We are talking about theatre, not about philosophy. The rationality of an audience is not specifically philosophical. For the philosopher, the excitement of working out ideas or having them come to him in a flash is indeed a livingness—and independent of their content or truth—but the more general and diffuse rationality of an audience shares in the delight of speculation only occasionally—in passages of Aristophanes and Shaw, for example. Allowing for some excursions of the kind, the center of gravity, the *querencia*, of audience rationality is mere good sense, a sort of informal logic.

MARCELINO

But how about its pleasure in formulated thought, in epigrams, paradoxes, and pat retorts?

DON RAFAEL

That would be entertainment only, I think, unless the remarks are appreciably events in the play of a certain spirit and become, as it were, lyric. The remarks in Aristophanes or Marivaux or Congreve are not merely witty, gags in themselves, but figures in the ongoing music of those minds. The good sense of the audience can rise to that or, again, sink to the knowingness of summer comedy or boulevard theatre, where the off-color remarks can be very clever indeed but appeal to an inert knowingness in the audience, rather as sentimental theatre takes the most rudimentary feelings for granted. There are ambiguous cases for our students: is Feydeau lyric or merely boulevard farce? He can be played either way.

MARCELINO

I give you most of the range of comedy, and you have on your side that remark about life being a comedy for him who thinks and a tragedy for him who feels.

183

But have you any claims on tragedy, as objective or rational theatre?

DON RAFAEL
Yes, but they will go unrecognized. I claim the Oedipus. He is first and foremost a reasoning politician, certainly not a psychological case and hardly even a character. He is a benevolent and efficient monarch dealing with a national emergency and what he very reasonably thinks is a political intrigue. The play is almost entirely the course of his reasoning. Tragically, he is up against an unreasonable and arbitrary cosmos. Rationality does require the irrational for its functioning in the theatre—social irrationality or eccentricity in comedy, cosmic irrationality in tragedy. There are certainly feelings of great intensity in the Oedipus, but they are hardly determined by the souls of the characters, they are rationally adequate responses to perfectly objective situations. About all we can do with Oedipus as a soul is a will to be himself, that is, the rational solver of enigmas, or a will to be rational.

MARCELINO
And the audience?

DON RAFAEL
Even more so. It reaches a very ecstasy of objectivity. We must add to the mirror and balcony kinds a jury-box theatre.

MARCELINO
With the Greeks, at least. The *Furies* of Aeschylus may be the first plain instance, but most of the major figures in Greek tragedy have a case to plead, and plead it, as plausibly as possible in rational terms, whatever the pathos. I have to give you most of the Greeks. The Athenians notoriously had a passion for jury duty, and

the forms and feelings of the courts got into their theatre, as a good deal of theatricalism got into their courts. But if their theatre is essentially legalistic, concerned with Justice, and right and wrong, where is our livingness? If we are confined to moral types, objectively considered and rationally explaining themselves, what happens to the feelings, or intersubjectivity itself?

DON RAFAEL

You forget what we said, that objectivity is a function of the subjectivity and can be a passion, and a properly exhilarating passion. And in the theatre, as in court, the cases are not at all clear, justice is not evident or done in advance, we are in hot pursuit of it through a tangle of conflicting claims. Is the case of Agamemnon clear? Is that of Clytemnestra? Aigisthus has a very good case. Shelley thought the audience of tragedy, at least of his *The Cenci*, performed a "restless casuistry" about the rights and wrongs of the case. We may lay it down that objectivity is thus not only a passion, but a very active one in the theatre. It dominates the passions of the play, but the dominating is a moment by moment conquest, a continuing excitement in itself, which is added to the passions of the play, rather to the sympathy of the audience with those passions, contains them and allows them to be possessed and realized, so that whatever intensity may be lost to our sympathy—and it may be very little—is made up or more than made up by the triumphant sense of objectivity maintaining itself through impossible difficulties, and overriding the most violent passions.

MARCELINO

But if justice is not done? It rarely is done in tragedies, or lamely at best.

DON RAFAEL

The audience wills it to be done at least, but

185

the gods or Destiny reverse the decision, usually on a rather empty technicality. If the hero comes to a bad end, at least the objectivity of the audience is only put in its place. Its reward at the end may be the thrill of a narrow escape, or a last-minute reprieve.

MARCELINO

Perhaps the Athenians felt that way about it. But can one expect a contemporary audience to have a passion for jury duty or to extend its passion for objective legalistics beyond the usual courtroom drama into the larger and more undefined issues of real life?

DON RAFAEL

No. Your audience may like a little morality, bad characters and good characters, but not a restless casuistry about what they are, and rationality so long as it keeps to knowingness and takes no great risks. Beyond such inert objectivity, so to say, people want the irrational, to the point of madness and monstrosity. They will go to Strindberg happily enough these days, but not to Ibsen if they can help it. Nevertheless there are many tricks to this trade, and you might possibly lure an audience into a rationalizing adventure on the heroic or quixotic scale in the universe of the Absurd. You might do a kind of Oedipus in terms of a contemporary mythology.

MARCELINO

But contemporary mythology is Freudian.

DON RAFAEL

In our youth it was, but surely not now. In his time O'Neill could do a Freudian *Oresteia* convincingly enough, but now it is doubly dead, compounding two dead mythologies, psychology being the deader of the two.

MARCELINO

But there is, or there was, a subjective theatre

186

without psychology.

DON RAFAEL

I have to admit it. At the end of the nineteenth century, when Time was still the great myth, rather than Space, there was a theatre of pure temporality, in Chekhov. There you have temperaments, neither psychologies nor characters, suffering dissolution in what was Destiny then—the gradual and irreparable passage of Time. The only rationality possible is the counting of years, marking anniversaries, and so on.

MARCELINO

I cannot endure Chekhov, not for a minute.

DON RAFAEL

Naturally not. You want dramatic action. And, as the white clown, I scarcely want objectivity reduced to the clock and the calendar or how many versts the station is from the town. But Chekhov is great theatre if you can stand it, and a clear instance for theory. In its way it is even heroic theatre, for the temperaments are surely understood by the Russians as qualities of soul, and their unwillingness or willingness not to be goes on, not within Society, but in a cosmos whose very substance, at the *fin de siècle* was Time. It used to bother us that Chekhov has no social or political theory and does not present the futility of the declining landed class in Russia as if something should be done about it. But the scene is a universal one, Time, not merely political history or the everlasting country estate of Russian literature, and the characters are not so much social types as souls, and with a variety of heroism, a code of generosity and a vague will to be good, or nice, which belong indeed to that class but are radically human.

MARCELINO

As a Spaniard you have the usual fellow-

187

feeling for Russians, and to you the Chekhov characters might as well be Spanish, but they have always struck me, on the stage, as a random collection of harmless eccentrics, not very interesting and not even entertaining.

DON RAFAEL

So your general intent is not in phase with that of Chekhov. Or perhaps you cannot accept the flow of Bergsonian time as a mythology or a proscenium. Nor can the white clown. But surely the Harlequin is in charge of it, the variations of a number of different subjectivities— reckless, nostalgic, buoyant, sentimental, and so on— through the disintegrating element of Time. Theoretically, life can be perfectly well taken as just such a harlequinade, and Chekhov not only represents life as that but demands of the audience the agile subjectivity of a Harlequin, taking on the colors and moods of the different characters, yes, eccentric enough, like society sketches, as they occur and change. Why not Impressionism of this kind in the theatre, as well as in painting and the Proustian novel?

MARCELINO

Very well in its time, but not now.

DON RAFAEL

No doubt Impressionism is over, for the time being, but you should not forget how real it was, nor even neglect its resources. Under the inconstant surface of sentimental events, under the harlequinade, the capricious-ness and the whimsicality, is a common soul, a generic force under the freaks of the species.

MARCELINO

I have no doubt of it, but it is Russian. Whether the fraternal communality of souls comes from Greek Orthodox ritual or a Slavic tribalism, no matter, the Russians do have it, and it is the assumption of all their novels and the proscenium of their theatre. Very well. It makes for a spiritual unity through thick and thin, a massive participation in the oddest fantasies and perversities, as solidly one and continuous as Reason in the seventeenth century—

DON RAFAEL
And a more abundant source of livingness, not to say livingness itself at the source. It is something like the common soul of Elizabethan England or of Spain in our Golden Age—

MARCELINO
Except that in Chekhov the action is lacking, and the imperialism.

DON RAFAEL
At least he comes at the end of one imperialism and before the rise of another. But the unbounded space is there well enough and a sense of the cosmos, so the common soul has all the dimension it needs for heroic theatre, though its immediate motion is in or through the small moments of time.

MARCELINO
But it is not heroic theatre.

DON RAFAEL
One might say it is subjectively heroic, objectively not, or not in the manner of the Greeks, or Shakespeare, or Lope. But let us try to keep our kinds distinct at least and, whatever Chekhov may implicitly be for the common soul of Russia, call him a fine example of the theatre of cosmic temporality. Impressionism if you will.

MARCELINO
I do. I take its profound livingness on faith, as

historical fact or as something Russian, not something for the present in America.

Don Rafael

What would be an equivalent in America? What is your cosmos like? Is time really a dimension of it at all? You call it a Space Age, but what kind of space do you really live in and what do you do in it? There is a great deal of activity, there are happenings and events, but is there any action? And if there is any, does the common soul of your public participate in it? Does that common soul, supposing there is one, function as passion, as rationality, as temperament, as juridical prurience, as technological acumen—

Marcelino

Do you want me to answer all that?

Don Rafael

Not now, but if you write a real play you will be feeling your way through all those questions and hoping you have more or less plausible answers. Most likely you will not formulate them. They will just come up of themselves behind your text when the text feels true and complete.

Marcelino

With luck. But we were theorizing, and you asked about Time. We were agreed that Chekhovian time is not our kind of time. It is more passage than it is duration, and that may be what irritates me as a classicist, but why should it go against the contemporary sense of time, which does not really believe in duration?

Don Rafael

Perhaps because our sense of time now is not in the tempo of Chekhov. The flowingness of Bergsonian time, its adagio, is not possible to us, who live in catastrophic time, presto at least, and surely in a staccato phrasing of events rather than his legato. We live in a detached present, neglecting the past and taking no long view of the future. This is promising for you, since stage time is an intensified present even when the characters talk about the past or it is a very long play. You have that relation—the continuous material present of stage time and the catastrophic present of real time. Or it may be a confusion, like mixing up real life with the theatrical events.

MARCELINO
Perhaps, with too much happening in reality, nothing should happen on the stage, at least no catastrophes.

DON RAFAEL
Beckett has already managed that, and O'Neill did something like it in *The Iceman Cometh*, and Gertrude Stein in *Four Saints in Three Acts*. There is a theatre of simple existence, of a state. It can be a state of expectation, as in *Waiting for Godot* or *Endgame*, or a state of perdition, or a state of salvation and saintly bliss, but the actual stage time is pure duration, not passage nor, for that matter, a dimension of action, as in classical theatre.

MARCELINO
Very well, a simple duration, or time not passing or being used, but only existing, a field in which happenings may occur or not occur, where silence would not be a delay of anything but a basic expression of duration, interrupted once in a while by words. And space, I suppose, could be any existing space, not any particular place. We may do without scenery. But if we still have characters, what of them?

DON RAFAEL
They must be existences first of all. It has been

understood for some time that whatever is meant by the theatre of existence it need not be existentialist. Sartre can illustrate existentialist doctrine in quite naturalist theatre, and Ionesco, who may be said to belong to the theatre of existence, has little enough to do with Existentialism. So our characters must be existences but not existentialists necessarily, or understood in the terms of that philosophy. I think what we have on our hands is very like what you thought you discovered in Molière, like the self-love or self-will which underlies all his social types and gives them a strange kind of externality to the social intrigues they are engaged in, to the very roles they play. We need not adopt the moral and psychological mechanics of the seventeenth century, but our existent characters will have much the same externality to the happenings that seem to involve them, and even to themselves. As existences they will be, as it were, mere witnesses to the world and to themselves in it. Something like the Stranger of Camus, if you want to let the monads of Leibniz stay back in history where they belong.

MARCELINO

Are we back to souls again?

DON RAFAEL

In a very limited way, I think. We can scarcely assume the heroic soul, composed of grand passions, honor, or the desire to maintain its being in the face of Destiny and the Cosmos; nor can we do very much with the soul governed by its rational faculty, small or large, and character or psychology of any kind is largely incidental now or accidental. The essence of the character as existence would be its presence to the world and to itself. It is first and foremost a witness—not God's spy, nor a participant, nor a judge or juryman. We may still call it a soul. At least it is more than a consciousness in

192

any scientific or current sense.

MARCELINO

Is it bodily? Existence is surely of bodies, and this soul as a witness, if it is to be there, on hand, as an eye-witness, must be at least in a body.

DON RAFAEL

Of course. And I think the present exaggeration of the body, and especially the naked body, scandalous or not, is a sort of crash program for establishing a theatre of existences. I think it goes astray, since it loses the sense of bare existence in erotic activity, in excessive involvement, or in diverting entertainment, though it may sometimes succeed, as it did with you, in being a repellent kind of theatre, which at least enlivens the audience's awareness of its own existence, of being a witness to something that might come up in court.

MARCELINO

We are back to the audience again. It seems clear and even rudimentary that the audience is a witnessing existence, a sort of silent Greek chorus. It is that first of all, even if by sympathy or imagination it participates and loses track of itself as a witness. In this theatre of existence, I presume it does not, but in that case I think we must abandon your dogma of intersubjectivity. The witness of the audience would be objective, and we get simply entertainment—

DON RAFAEL

We might, but we often do not. From the beginning of theatre the witnessing function is not confined to the audience but exists on the stage, abundantly. Most obvious is the play within a play, not only in *Hamlet* and in *Six Characters in Search of An Author*, but in any play involving disguise or a mistaken identity there is a witnessing subjectivity behind the objective appearance. And any play with a deception in it—and how old that is!—makes both the audience and the deceiver witnesses to the deception. Comic or tragic, no matter, the theatrical instinct for keeping a clear distance between the subjectivity and the objective action seems to be eternal.

MARCELINO
Is it a kind of esthetic distance?

DON RAFAEL
No. Esthetic distance is a kind of it, a special kind of the radical distance or decalage in real life between the subjectivity and its objects, which the Existentialists have sufficiently explicated. The distance between the characters in a play and their action, realized by soliloquies, mad scenes, disguises and so on, is of course not esthetic. It may be used for the exhibition of a subjectivity distinct from its action, or of the motivations distinct from the event, even of psychology and character, but in the theatre of existence it would simply assert the bare existence of the subjectivities of the characters. And those subjectivities should not do much more than exist, however lively the action, so that there is a continuously clear correspondence between the bare or unqualified existence of the subjectivities of the characters and the subjectivities of the audience. Am I making myself clear?

MARCELINO
Only intermittently, to me, Don Rafael.

DON RAFAEL
You were once a good student. But to recapitulate. Once upon a time there was a theatre of full souls passionately realizing themselves in a great big expansive cosmos.

MARCELINO
One.

DON RAFAEL
Then there was a theatre of more or less
rational characters trying to get what they wanted in a
practical way within a fairly well regulated and settled
society.

MARCELINO
Two.

DON RAFAEL
Then there was a theatre of sensitive and
variable personalities gradually dissolving in the element
of Time as passage.

MARCELINO
Three.

DON RAFAEL
And now we have, well under way, a theatre
of bare subjective existences witnessing whatever there is
or whatever is done. As to time, they pass it. As to space
and place, they are anywhere, where they happen to be.

MARCELINO
And as to what they are?

DON RAFAEL
We have called them witnesses. We could
call them unconditional subjectivities. That would make
them pure negation or not-being for some existentialist
Theory, but we once agreed, with Plato to back us up, that
not-being is something, and a not-being which functions as
a witness is a something in spades. Among my clowns there
was a blue one, with spangles, which we compared in a
poetizing moment to a night sky.

MARCELINO

He was a symbol of intersubjectivity, but so, in a way, was the white clown, when the theatre was an objectivity performing in common, and so was the Harlequin.

DON RAFAEL

They were conditional—the subjectivity committed to action and objective interests or, in the case of the Harlequin, to its own variations in Time. Our blue clown is not so committed, or looks on at those commitments. Perhaps it is too much to call him unconditional subjectivity, but we still might call him the subjectivity as witness to its external conditions, or as previous to them. He is essentially withdrawn and in a solitude, at the extreme edge of existence, not in the thick of it like the other clowns. Such a solitary and naked subjectivity is in everyone. Do you agree?

MARCELINO

Yes. It is constantly asserted by religions and many philosophies, but also an intuition that everyone has about his own life, at least at times. Anyway, let me agree.

DON RAFAEL

Good, because we can come to the real difficulty, which is how such a solitary existence becomes a ground of intersubjectivity. We agree that it is in everyone and we may suppose it is nearly identical in everyone, like the self-love of the seventeenth century, but how do two or more solitudes communicate, directly and as solitudes? And in the theatre? You mentioned the sort of vibration set up in Molière's theatre by the sudden acts of anarchic self-will by perfectly conventional and social characters. That vibration may be the kind of communication between or among solitary existences we are after—not sympathy as in the theatre of passion or the common rationality of comedy.

MARCELINO

I hope it is. I really do not like sympathy in the theatre. It is usually maudlin, a parasitic or vicarious emotion, always on the verge of a general *Schwärmerei*. And I think generally now it is felt to be sentimentality and not enough. As rationality is also felt to be rather idle. But a sense of isolated existences, previous to any particular passion or reasoning, and certainly, now, with no *raison d'être* behind them or ahead of them, must be clear in almost everyone.

DON RAFAEL

Well, if not clear it is being clarified. The human condition is constantly being lectured upon in those terms on the stage, even by Beckett. But once the doctrine has subsided into a tacit assumption we may have a pure theatre of existence, not a didactic explanation or demonstration of the concept of existence.

MARCELINO

If we get a collection of monads in the house and a group of monads on stage, all within the rigid pre-established harmony of stage time and of theatre space, and all about identical in their aspect of solitary and contingent existence, any stage event expressing such existence or expressing anything from the point of view of such existence, ought to have an automatic repercussion or vibration in each existence or monad in the house.

DON RAFAEL

Yes, and quite as anything touching honor or the will to be rang clearly in each member of the Spanish audience. But notice that if bare existence is the substance of your audience and the stage event alike, character and morals are incidental if not insignificant, action is irrelevant, or a diversion, and the passions only a rather colorful entertainment, like stage business or a light show. Only a few passions relating to bare existence—bliss, horror, indifference, irony—will really carry. Love, ambition, honor, and so on, any passion which tries to transcend existence, will be an absurdity—to be taken as comic or tragic, as the playwright prefers—but not provoking the deepest response or sympathy of the audience. Under our night sky, under the sign of the blue clown, who implies all of outer somethingness around the single existence, its pretentions to anything more than existence are curiosities.

MARCELINO

It sounds like an impossible theatre—no morals, no characters, no passions to speak of—

DON RAFAEL

It is quite possible, since it is being done, or in process of creation. There is a lot of it you do not like, the orgiastic stuff with naked bodies, the systematic use of ugliness to flout conventional beauty, the disorderly or chance use of visual and auditory shocks, the senseless or incomprehensible activity, the rather monotonous use of negation, with rare appearances of any clown but our red one. But all of that is working toward establishing a theatre of existence, more empirically than theoretically setting up a proscenium or frame of reference which is simply human existence. Or it is trying to abstract from life at large a plane of exhibition which can no longer be the plane of continuous action, or Being, or Destiny, or Society, or Passage, but must be simply the duration of existence.

MARCELINO

But if the plane of bare existence is set up it seems to be a very empty plane, without interest. If it is, as you said, a plane of exhibition, evidently its interest will depend on what is exhibited on it.

DON RAFAEL

Rather the other way round. The material of the theatre, human living, is fairly constant, but its interest depends on the plane on which it is expressed. If we believe Aristotle, the Greeks set up a plane of action, and the interest of the material expressed on it, human living, depended on the expression of the active aspect of human living being articulated on that plane—"people doing something," as he says. In Shakespearean theatre we get people being something, inside and out, as well as doing something. In social theatre we get people behaving themselves. And in Impressionist theatre we get people gradually ceasing to be anything, on the plane of Passage. There is nothing wrong with any of these planes except that we do not really live on them. They belong to history or to past works of art. By imagination we can accept them as conventions and enjoy whatever goes on upon them esthetically. Once in a while they seem to intersect the plane of existence on which we live, and there is a startling moment of life in them. But a theatre of existence can and should aspire to a much more continuous and direct livingness by referring all its materials—action, passion, behavior, dissolution, and the like—as constantly as it can to its own plane.

MARCELINO

I don't see it.

DON RAFAEL

I do. We are in the rudimentary stages of it, in spite of the extraordinary accomplishments of Beckett, and the theatre has all it can do just establishing its plane, rather as Cézanne had all he could do in his own terms and could not get on to Cubism. But I do see that, once the plane is established and clarified, then the devices for making even the most intractable material articulate upon it will be invented or evolved or—as with soliloquy, masks, disguises, and deceptions—adapted from the past. And I see above all that the white clown of objective action, the diabolical red clown, and the Harlequin of individual subjectivity, will all be excellent straight men for the blue clown, who will speak for us all.

MARCELINO
In verse or prose?

DON RAFAEL
I do not see or hear that clearly. But probably verse, since he is alone, like an arch-monad, and hence lyric. He may sing like a Greek chorus, lamenting or rejoicing over what he witnesses.

MARCELINO
Or like the Fool in *Lear?*

DON RAFAEL
Yes, but let us not dwell on the past appearances of the blue clown. He has rarely been the lead. Now I think he will be.

MARCELINO
Is there a reason for that?

DON RAFAEL
No doubt, but for your purposes, if you still have them, the main reason is the practical one—where to take hold of the audience, and as action, ideas, issues, and so on do not really hold the audience but only entertain it, you take hold of what is left, its bare human existence. Just now it is more grabbed than taken hold of, but that will change.

MARCELINO
But its bare existence is static, constant, if you prefer. Even if it is a force, a gravitation to presence,

it is largely inert, or non-dramatic. Should it be kept so, or does one present very violent activity to it in order to get it moving, participating in the livingness of the stage events?

Don Rafael

We once said livingness can be in the maintaining of stillness, and a very intense livingness indeed may be in a lack of liveliness. But in life we have a great deal of violence, and I do not know whether that will mean violence or calm in the coming theatre.

Marcelino

Perhaps an inner violence?

Don Rafael

Perhaps. I do not see that far. And it is your problem.

Marcelino

So you leave it to me? Or to others?

Don Rafael

Yes. As I said, the future is not my affair. And yet, yes, I will begin to think about it.

A Note about the Authors

Augusto Centeno y Rilova was born in 1901, in Ronda, a dramatic Andalusian city divided by a gorge so deep it has three seasons going at once. In one branch of his family had been Teresa of Avila and other saints. He was educated by the University of Madrid, where one of his teachers was Ortega y Gasset, and Federico Garcia Lorca and Luis Buñuel were his classmates. Salvador Dali was around. But much of his manner, in thought and conversation, was formed in the *tertulia* of Ramón Gomez de la Serna at the Café de Pombo, a kind of headquarters of the modern movement in Madrid at the time.

In 1921 he left Spain and began teaching at Princeton. In 1933 a sophomore, Donald Sutherland, accidentally took a course in second-year Spanish from him. He learned much more than Spanish, and an essential way of knowing everything he was ever to know. From a casual student he became almost at once a disciple, with not much mind of his own. Born in 1915 in Seattle, Donald Sutherland was more exactly a native of the Yukon Valley, where his father was prospecting, so his attraction to a great Andalusian mind with saints behind it was polar and complete.

The quarrels were not about ideas, the disciple remained a disciple, and felt he might plausibly complete a few of the projects left in the notes of his late master. Besides, the projects were in part a general inheritance from the masters in Madrid—not only Ortega y Gasset but Gomez de la Serna, whose agile and glittering book on the Circus was the source of several projects for dialogues, with the clowns transposed to critical categories.

Here is one page of the pencilled notes:

ESTETICA DEL TEATRO
INTERLOCUTORES:
Colaborador Primero – Don Rafael. Ex-profesor, ciego.
voc. Maestro
Colaborador Segundo – Marcelino. Antiguo alumno suyo y
sucesor. voc. Colaborador, ayudante,
amigo, hijo, secretario, alumno.

And here are some notes for his last lecture, ending a course in Esthetics he gave at Connecticut College:

What have we really achieved? I don't know. It's very difficult to determine at this point.

We have come to the end of the journey.

Fasten your seat belts.

And don't forget to put on your shoes.

Good-bye and good luck.

D. S.